The Lymans of Hawai'i Island

A Pioneering Family

The shade of the Lyman Mission House offers a cool harbor on a warm Hilo afternoon. It takes a minute for your eyes to adjust fully, to let the past move into the present. When you look about at the artifacts of daily life of a century and a half ago, you cannot help but recognize that the New Englanders who came in the 19th century had every intention of recreating their past on this distant island. There is a spare, durable, utilitarian quality here that echoes the same hard dreams of those who colonized Plymouth and New Bedford over the preceding two centuries.

The silence of the old Mission House is broken next door, by the excitement of a modern museum, with programs for residents, visitors, Elderhostel groups and fascinated schoolchildren. It is the legacy of a family who—over five generations now—have put their community first.

The Lymans of Hawai'i Island
A Pioneering Family

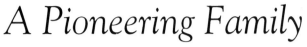

Written, edited and produced by
MacKinnon Simpson

Researched and original manuscript by
Helen Baldwin

Designed by
Malinda Abell

Photography by
Mark T. Watanabe, C.P.P.

The Lyman family Coat of Arms

PUBLISHER:
ORLANDO H. LYMAN TRUST
276 Haili Street
Hilo, Hawai'i 96720 (808) 935-5021

Library of Congress Catalog
Card Number 93-087496
ISBN: 0-945367-99-6
Hard cover trade edition

Printed in Hong Kong

First trade edition, November 1993

The Lymans of Hawai'i Island
A Pioneering Family

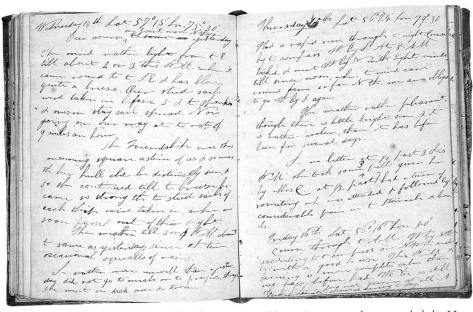

David Lyman's shipboard journal for the voyage to Hawai'i, just as they rounded the Horn.

Islands of Fire

It seems hard to believe today, as jetliners from around the world slice through Hawai'i's skies, and satellites in space transmit everything from weather to HBO down to earth stations below, but the Hawaiian Islands are the most remote landform on the face of the earth. More remote even than lonely Pitcairn or frigid Antarctica.

Twenty-five million years ago, at the very end of what geologists call the Oligocene Epoch, a crack appeared in the sea floor of the Central North Pacific. Molten magma gurgled into the cold, black water some two miles below the surface, solidifying and rising, solidifying and rising, for hundreds of thousands of years, until it finally burst from the ocean swells into the atmosphere, an island at last. The

Facing Page: December 1824. Converted by the missionaries, high chiefess Kapi'olani stands at the edge of Halema'uma'u Crater taunting Pele by saying, "Jehovah is my God. He kindled these fires. I fear not Pele. If I perish in her anger, then you may fear Pele; but if I trust in Jehovah, then you must fear and serve Him alone." The old religion was broken, its priesthood's power shattered.

process continues still, both on the Island of Hawai'i and beneath the sea to the south, where a submerged island-to-be named Lō'ihi Seamount is imperceptibly but inexorably taking shape.

The Hawaiian archipelago was originally settled by ancient Polynesians, who followed the stars and swells in their fragile, carved wooden canoes from their home islands in the South Seas. The earliest explorers to discover Hawai'i—the accepted date is now 450AD, though it may be substantially earlier—were part of one of the epic achievements of mankind: The Peopling of the Polynesian Triangle. These early voyagers found and settled every habitable bit of land in some sixteen million square miles of ocean, an area with but two units of land for every thousand of water, at a time when Europeans were fearful of sailing over the horizon.

For perhaps thirteen centuries, these people existed in splendid isolation from the rest of the world, worshiping their Gods, fighting their wars, raising their families. Their society was complex and ecologically balanced, with ocean fishing seasons, sophisticated aquaculture and a land/ocean resource management system called *ahupua'a*.

One day in 1778, two Royal Navy ships hove over the horizon, and that

9

This image of Captain Cook at a feast in his honor at a heiau has been cited as evidence that the Hawaiians believed Cook was the reincarnation of Lono, one of their major deities. ABCFM missionary Sheldon Dibble was especially vociferous in his denunciations of Cook, though whether Cook was actually considered Lono—and/or knowingly accepted being mistaken for a god—will probably forever remain a mystery.

isolation was shattered forever. Captain James Cook had spent the better part of the past decade discovering, exploring and meticulously charting the islands of the Pacific, and now, on his way to search for the elusive Northwest Passage, he came across Hawai'i.

In Cook's own words, penned in his shipboard journal, it was "...a discovery which, though the last, seemed in many respects to be the most important that have hitherto been made by Europeans throughout the extent of the Pacific Ocean."

Familiar with Pacific tongues from Easter Island to New Zealand, James Cook immediately realized the Hawaiians were of Polynesian stock and so must have discovered these islands by canoe. As the most accomplished explorer and navigator in the Western world, Cook understood well the enormity of the settlement of Polynesia and wrote in his journal. "How shall we account for this nation having spread itself to so many detached islands so widely disjoined from each other in every quarter of the Pacific Ocean? What we now already know in consequence of this voyage warrants our pronouncing it to be, by far, the most extensive nation on Earth."

Cook's three voyages correctly mapped the Pacific for the first time. But they had a second, more anthropological impact, for these explorations were planned by the Royal Society and were very much like present-day National Geographic expeditions. Aboard were scientists of many stripes—botanists, astronomers, naturalists—plus an official voyage artist. What we now know of Hawaiian society at the moment of contact is the result of the detailed observations and drawings made by these people, including Captain Cook.

First contact, at Kaua'i in January 1778, was but a few days, for Cook had a small window of summer weather in which to proceed north and explore the Arctic. Almost a year later, on a return visit to the Islands, the two ships spent several weeks moored at Kealakekua Bay on the Island of Hawai'i. This was an important Hawaiian settlement, and the English carefully recorded every detail.

Captain James Cook lost his life on the shore at Kealakekua. The voyage's second-in-command, Captain Charles Clerke, placed the blame for Cook's death squarely upon Cook himself, who with a contingent of ten armed Royal Marines, had barged headlong into an enormous crowd of Hawaiians and tried to take the ruling chief, Kalani'ōpu'u, hostage so as to force the return of a small boat.

The voyage continued as planned, but without Cook, whose mortal remains lay buried at sea in Kealakekua Bay. In late 1780, the ships arrived home in England, and the journals and charts and maps were published, disclosing the existence of what Cook had called the Sandwich Islands, in honor of his long-time patron, the Earl of Sandwich.

One of the enormous side-effects of the publication of the voyage journals was the establishment of a Pacific Fur Trade, for when the ships had anchored in the Northwest, the Indians there had given Cook's men luxurious sea otter pelts, that later fetched $100 each (in 1779 dollars) when the voyagers stopped at Macao.

The Chinese were the key to trade in the Pacific at this time, for they had

During his lifetime, Kamehameha I was known as Tamehameha, and he died before the missionaries arrived and simplified the language. Artist-historian Herb Kāne painted this image of what he looked like about 1790.

tea and spices, porcelains and silks, all extremely valuable in Europe. Finding a trade item that these merchants desired was a profitable discovery, and English ships were soon outfitted for this new fur trade. Within a few years, guided by Cook's charts, the first fur traders stopped at the Sandwich Islands for provisions on their way between the Northwest and China. While they were in the Islands, the fur traders recruited Hawaiians to hunt otters in the Northwest and also traded for water, fresh food and firewood.

In one of the loads of firewood, it is supposed, some fragrant sandalwood—called 'iliahi by the Hawaiians—was carried aboard. This was even more valuable to the Chinese (and hence to the traders) than the furs, which were running out anyway, so the fur traders soon shifted to filling their holds with sandalwood. The Islands, too, suddenly shifted from an occasional provisioner of water and yams to an on-going provider of a profitable commodity.

A young chief on Hawai'i Island, Kamehameha, wanted to consolidate his hold there and bring the other islands

The Foreign Mission School in Cornwall, Connecticut was founded by the American Board of Commissioners for Foreign Missions in 1816. Its goal was to prepare foreign youths—like Henry Obookiah—to return to their native lands where they could augment or replace American missionaries who were already (or in Hawai'i's case, soon would be) serving there.

Originally entitled "A Missionary Preaching to the Natives, under a Skreen of plaited Cocoa-nut leaves at Kairua," this image was done in 1823 by English missionary William Ellis. David Lyman—who was then a college student—would later repeat this scene many times as he travelled around Hawai'i Island. These buildings are part of a school and church complex.

under his control. He shrewdly traded his sandalwood for Western weapons and ships and eventually became the first monarch to rule all the islands.

Kamehameha I was a strict but enlightened ruler. As a young *ali'i*, he had gone aboard Cook's ships and years later had become good friends with George Vancouver, an English explorer who had accompanied Cook and later commanded a Pacific voyage of his own. Kamehameha had both English and American advisors, who helped him in battle and later to reign. From pre-contact with the West to post-contact, Kamehameha I is the transitional figure in Hawaiian history.

Hawai'i's first true king, he was also the last to practice the old religion and enforce the old social order. The ancient religion, with its panoply of four major

deities, had been brought intact on the canoes from Tahiti. It shaped every aspect of the Polynesian culture and society.

As contact with Western ships increased—those of traders and explorers primarily—adventurous Hawaiians began to travel to lands far away. In 1809, a young orphan named 'Ōpūkaha'ia from the village of Nāpo'opo'o boarded the ship *Triumph*, bound for New Haven, Connecticut. According to legend he was found, lonely and crying, by a student named Edwin Dwight, on the stone steps of Yale College. Dwight befriended 'Ōpūkaha'ia and introduced him to Samuel Mills, a member of the Haystack Experience, a group of pious young men who had taken refuge in a haystack during a thunderstorm and experienced a profound religious conversion.

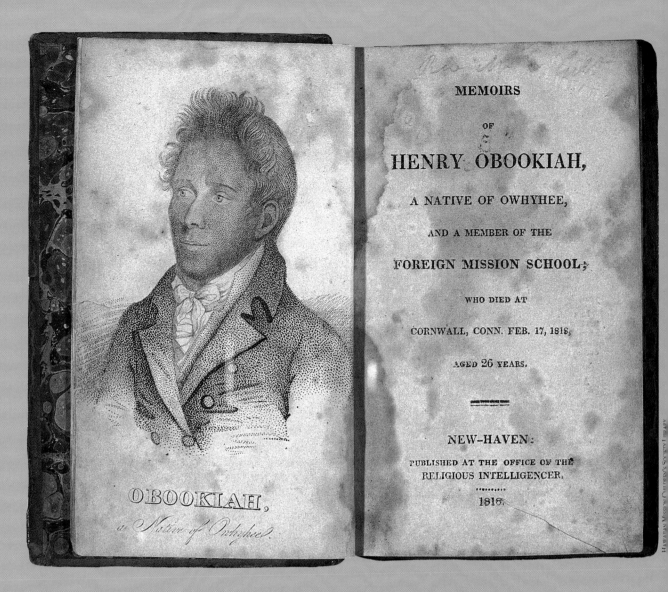

MEMOIRS

OF

HENRY OBOOKIAH,

A NATIVE OF OWHYHEE,

AND A MEMBER OF THE

FOREIGN MISSION SCHOOL;

WHO DIED AT

CORNWALL, CONN. FEB. 17, 1818,

AGED 26 YEARS.

⸺

NEW-HAVEN:

PUBLISHED AT THE OFFICE OF THE
RELIGIOUS INTELLIGENCER.
....
1818.

OBOOKIAH,
a Native of Owhyhee.

Henry Obookiah was the catalyst whose deep faith—and untimely death—inspired creation of the Sandwich Islands Mission. His shining eyes gazed brightly from this first edition of his Memoirs, though by the time this was printed Henry himself was but a memory. But this young orphan's death, in a New England winter six thousand miles from his Island homeland, did not go unnoticed. In fact, this thin little volume begat a revolution that would not be stilled until the bearers of Christianity had prevailed.

Poor, cold Henry became a symbol for the missionary movement—a symbol of ignorance in search of fulfillment, of the heathen in need of enlightenment.

His headstone in Cornwall Cemetery reads:

In Memory of HENRY OBOOKIAH a native of OWYHEE His arival in this country gave rise to the Foreign mission school of which he was a worthy member. He was once an Idolater and was designed for a Pagan Priest; but by the grace of God and by the prayers and instructions of pious friends, he became a christian. He was eminent for piety and missionary Zeal. When almost prepared to return to his native Isle, to preach the Gospel, God took to himself. In his last sickness he wept and prayed for Owhyhee, but was submissive. He died without fear with a heavenly smile on his countenance and glory in his soul Feb 17, 1818, aged 26.

'Ōpūkaha'ia told them of seeing his parents killed when he was ten and being raised by an uncle, a *kahuna* (priest) in the traditional religion. He also told of ferocious battles waged by Kamehameha and of *kapu* (taboos) punishable by death. 'Ōpūkaha'ia soon converted to Christianity—the first Hawaiian to do so—and was baptized Henry Obookiah, about as close a phonetic pronunciation as the New Englanders could manage. He convinced his new friends that the Hawaiian people needed Christianity, and enrolled at the new Foreign Mission School in Cornwall, Connecticut, where he was trained as the first missionary destined for the Islands. He died of typhus in 1818, before his plans were realized, but the posthumous publication of his melodramatic—and wildly popular—*Memoirs* incited the American Board of Commissioners for Foreign Missions to establish a missionary company bound for the Islands.

1819 was a pivotal year in Hawai'i history. In May, a pair of New England whaleships arrived in Hawaiian waters, portending an invasion of whalers that would last through the 1870s and change these Islands, economically and socially, forever.

In September, Kamehameha the Great died. His eldest son Liholiho—now Kamehameha II—inherited his father's name but not his Greatness. Within a few months, the Hawaiians' traditional religion, and the complex social system it supported, had been destroyed.

In late October, a Company of Protestant missionaries left Boston in the brig *Thaddeus*, chartered by the American Board. These seven young couples were bound for the Sandwich Islands, where they expected to find Kamehameha and his powerful priesthood resisting them. Instead they found a vacuum—a land suddenly devoid of its centuries-old religion and a native people willing to listen to them.

After some difficult negotiations, Kamehameha II granted these first missionaries a probationary year to start their churches and introduce their new God. After that first year, they were allowed to remain, and more ABCFM missionaries arrived in the Islands. By 1832, four separate "Companies" had come and a Fifth was en route. Many of these men and women came and served for a time, then returned to New England for reasons of poor health, personal choice, and—in at least one case—a determination of unfit to serve. Others resigned from their calling but stayed in the Islands as businessmen and/or government officials.

A few remained missionaries here all their lives, devoting themselves selflessly to the tasks at hand. One such pair was in the Fifth Company: David Belden Lyman and his bride of a few months, Sarah Joiner Lyman.

The Lymans never returned to New England, not even for a visit. They never moved from their original Mission in Hilo, where they established a boy's training school that operated for close to a century. Many Lyman descendants have made Hawai'i their home and have contributed greatly to the community down through the 150 years plus since their pious ancestors first arrived.

New England & Its People

Nature of her boundless store
Threw rocks together
and no more.

— early Yale President Ezra Stiles,
on New England

The New England which greeted colonists arriving from Europe in the 1600s was a harsh place, often still described by residents as "nine months of winter and three months of damn poor sledding." Granite hills had been scoured clean by glacial fingers scrubbing a path south during the last Ice Age. As the glacier melted and receded,

Left: Royalton, Vermont, 2AM, November 3, 1831: As family and friends wish them well, newlyweds Rev. and Mrs. David Belden Lyman climb aboard a Concord coach for their journey to Boston, the first leg on an 18,000 mile trip to Hilo, Hawai'i.

The Lyman's son Henry described the scene in his book, Hawaiian Yesterdays: "The snow flakes flew, the winds of Winter wept and wailed among the branches of the maples and elms, as the muddy stage coach rolled up to the door at two o'clock in the morning, and bore away the young couple from the home and the friends who gave up that sweet bride. Farewell, farewell, father, mother, sister, brothers dear! A long farewell indeed! for they were never to meet on earth again."

it deposited rocks and boulders and gravel, turning New England into a huge moraine. The early colonists settled along the rocky coast, where they established prosperous shipbuilding and fishing industries. Others slowly worked their way inland along the rivers, which provided transportation and power. They found the land coated with a thick forest primeval. Sinewed men swinging double-bladed axes from morning till night cleared ever-expanding rectangles, allowing unfiltered sunlight to reach the ground for the first time in centuries. The short growing season made small family subsistence farms the norm, for this was not plantation country. With levers, fire and oxen, huge stumps were pried from their tenacious grip in the earth. Rocks were belly-lugged to wooden sleds and trundled off to be tossed into mounded walls, though each winter the deep frosts would heave more to the surface to be cleared again in the spring and added to the walls. New England's beloved poet laureate, Robert Frost, once noted that his father had "strung chains of wall round everything."

Colonists arriving from England named the area New England after their home country, and they named their settlements—New Hampshire, New Bedford, New London—after towns and

An itinerant circuit rider and his steed brave the elements as they carry the Word to remote towns and settlements along the early frontier. The scene is reminiscent of David Lyman's description of his early journeys up and down the Hāmākua Coast.

cities back home.

Or at least in what used to be back home. For most early New England colonists were escapees—people originally from the British Isles who had serious differences of opinion with the Crown. The official—and officious— religion in Great Britain at that time was Anglicanism, a sort of British Catholicism without a Pope. Most of the people who moved to the colonies were Protestants of one ilk or another—out of favor with, and often persecuted by, their government.

The colonies, which the British government saw as a source of prosperity and a provider of products, were tolerant of religious freedom. This decision was both a political and economic one—it eliminated unpopular believers at home where they were a source of controversy and sent them to the colonies where they could worship however they wanted so long as they provided a source of labor to increase the wealth of the Mother Country.

The colonists saw their situation differently. According to a prophecy by Edward Johnson, as Olde England declined, New England was "the place where the Lord will create a new heaven and a new earth." These people had a destiny, a mission, and believed they were soldiers in the Army of Christ, selected to create the perfect world. Many of these people were indeed, in their own minds and in the biblical sense, Pilgrims.

The Protestant religion was, by its very name, born of protest. Its roots were in the Reformation, a movement started by a German monk named Martin Luther in the early 1500s to reform the bloated and top-heavy Catholic church. One of Luther's followers, John Calvin, proposed that each church be ruled by a council of its own elders rather than a centralized authority. Calvin stressed the holiness of thrift, hard work and conservation of resources. This has come down to us as the "Puritan work ethic" and is a heritage of New Englanders even today.

Since Protestantism, by definition, encouraged autonomy, there were many fringe sects—Puritans, Presbyterians, Congregationalists, Quakers and Baptists among them. English Calvinists were called Puritans because they wanted to "purify" the Anglican Church of, among other things, its bishop. All were fiercely independent. Edmund Burke, the most influential British politician of his day, described the colonists: "The people are Protestants, and of that kind which is most adverse to all implicit subjection of mind and opinion."

Born of dispute with authority, the religious heritage of the colonists led to questioning of the British crown at many turns. Over the course of a century and a half, it would eventually lead to a formal Declaration of Independence and then a fierce war of independence.

In colonial New England, the Congregationalists (who got their name from a belief that each congregation was a complete church unto itself) far outnumbered all other sects. While their early ministers came from England, the next batch was home-grown, and Harvard (in 1636) and Yale (in 1701) were both founded to educate Congregationalist clergy.

Not everyone was a churchgoer, certainly, but these beliefs formed the basis of an almost universal philosophy. In 1740, a fire-breathing itinerant preacher named George Whitefield tramped the countryside and gathered crowds in fields and on town commons for revival meetings. Almost single-handedly, Whitefield created The Great Awakening, an evangelical fervor which convinced many colonists that they had indeed been chosen by God for a special mission.

The Great Awakening crossed over denominational lines—a shared experience which became a shared concept. It took religion from the head—where it had migrated during the Age of Reason—to the heart. It was more than a burst of revival fervor, and in fact, contributed mightily, if unintentionally, to the political revolution which would follow. The Great Awakening blurred differences between denominations and created a unity of thought among a majority of colonists.

By this time, most colonists were second- and third- and sometimes fourth-generation New Englanders. They had been busy conquering Nature—evicting Indians, taming a wilderness, building homes and mills and towns.

Yet they still retained a sense of independence, both of religion and of self. Their churches were often called "meeting houses" to carefully distinguish

them from the elaborate places of worship of Catholics and Anglicans. And meeting houses they truly were, especially in the small rural villages. The American Revolution was created and sustained in these meeting houses—and taverns—of the New World.

New England, the nurturer of Religious defiance of the Crown, was also the birthplace of colonial defiance at England's rule, a defiance that bred such hotheads as Samuel Adams and Thomas Paine. These colonists objected to what they perceived as a vast array of English injustices towards them. Very early on, in 1605, a Captain Weymouth of the Royal Navy discovered stands of white pine in New England stretching well over 100' tall. Growing in tight groves and striving for sunlight, these trees were straight and

THE AMERICAN BOARD of COMMISSIONERS for FOREIGN MISSIONS

From its very roots—twelve disciples two thousand years ago—efforts to convert non-believers have characterized Christianity. Through the centuries, Christian missionaries have spread the Gospel around the world.

The same idealistic young people who today might join the Peace Corps, Greenpeace or Earthtrust, instead became missionaries in the 1800s, and a surprisingly high proportion of college-educated men were ordained.

In 19th century New England, young men and women were abandoning the cities and seaports and hardscrabble hill-farms to strike out on their own. Many headed for the frontier, or went off

whaling. Others went into ship-building or manufacturing. Altruistic young people turned toward missionary work.

The earliest missionaries went from New England on their own or supported by wealthy parishes, often targeting Indians on reservations for conversion. But the New England missionary effort crystallized with the creation of the American Board of Commissioners for Foreign Missions (right) in 1810. The ABCFM sent a total of twelve companies with 159 missionaries plus ten Hawaiians and two Tahitians to the Sandwich Islands between 1819 and 1844. A few other Protestant missionaries came independently.

the wood was strong, light and easily worked—perfect for ship's masts for the Royal Navy. England sent Royal Mast Agents into the forests to slash the King's Broad Arrow into trees—those more than 24" in girth and close to the sea—reserved exclusively for the Crown. This practice, and the Stamp Act and high taxes on tea, fueled a resentment that finally became a revolution.

The success of that Revolution—when a loose band of farmers defeated the greatest power on Earth—convinced many of an unspoken tenet which lasted at least through World War II: God is on our side. The victory reinforced the colonists' inherent belief in the moral superiority of "their" American system. They were willing—eager even—to share this better society with others, and

American missionaries brought with them not only Christ, but a way of living that they were absolutely certain had been approved, personally, by God.

It was into this New England that David Lyman and Sarah Joiner were born and raised. Both were from old New England families, but from very different places. David was born in 1803 at the New Hartford, Connecticut family farm, an eighth-generation Lyman in America. His ancestors had left England for the New World in 1631—just eleven years after the Mayflower Pilgrims landed at Plymouth Rock.

When they departed High Ongar in Essex County, England to make their home in the American colonies, Richard Lyman, his wife Sarah and their five children were landed gentry. In America,

Dᵣ Wisner.   Jeremiah Evarts.   Dᵣ Worcester.   Dᵣ Cornelius.   Dᵣ Armstrong.

DECEASED SECRETARIES OF THE AMERICAN BOARD OF COMMISSIONERS FOR FOREIGN MISSIONS.

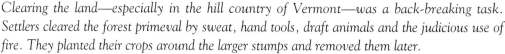

Clearing the land—especially in the hill country of Vermont—was a back-breaking task. Settlers cleared the forest primeval by sweat, hand tools, draft animals and the judicious use of fire. They planted their crops around the larger stumps and removed them later.

they purchased land from some Indians— probably the Pocumtucks—near New Hartford. David's grandfather fought in the Revolution and ran a grist mill along a riverbank, and his father farmed nearby.

By the time David had arrived, Connecticut, Massachusetts and Rhode Island had become crowded, at least by the standards of the day. Families were often large, as the tremendous amount of

work to be done far outweighed the minimal cost of feeding another mouth. Children often moved elsewhere when they grew up, as there was no longer room for them on the family homestead. This was not the case with Sarah's birthplace, about 150 miles to the north, in rural Vermont.

Sarah was born in 1805, on a hill farm outside Royalton, a sixth-generation

New Englander. Vermont had been settled only a few generations before, by people moving into the Grants from the more crowded areas to the South. It had been home to the indomitable Revolutionary heroes, Ethan Allen and his Green Mountain Boys, and Vermonters had a fierce reputation for notorious independence. In a 1777 territorial dispute between New York and New Hampshire, Vermont actually declared itself a separate country—the Republic of the Green Mountains. For some fourteen years, this tiny nation issued its own laws, stamps and currency, much to the chagrin of President George Washington, who once actually suggested (and then later thought better of) invasion.

Sarah's grandfather was an original settler of Royalton, in the foothills of the Green Mountains for which Verd (green) Mont (mountain) is named. The town is situated along the White River, a tributary of the Connecticut, New England's most important waterway, which cuts a swath from the Canadian border south to the Long Island Sound.

Sarah was a farmer's daughter and a farmer's granddaughter. Her family was prosperous enough to see that she had a good education, especially for a girl in those days. She graduated from Royalton Academy, then made a memorable trip to Boston to visit some relatives. There she

An early New England farm scene. This lithograph shows a typical family farm and, save for the difference in terrain—the hills of Vermont vs. the flatlands of Connecticut—it would have been very similar to the ones on which both Sarah and David grew up.

> This may certify, that the intention of marriage between David B. Lyman of New Hartford Con. & Sarah Joiner of Royalton Ver. was read in public meeting at the former place October 23, 1831, & that the way was thus prepared for the parties to be legally married, according to the statutes of Connecticut, at any subsequent time.
>
> Cyrus Yale
> Pastor of the Cong. Church.
>
> New Hartford
> Oct. 26, 1831.

"Wedding bans" served as a public announcement that a couple planned to marry. This document was, in effect, a marriage license, recognized "according to the statutes of Connecticut," and issued by David's local pastor, Cyrus Yale.

attended church services devoted to foreign missions and was filled with three things: the desire to do missionary work, a doubt that she was worthy, and fear that no opportunity would arise. Back in Royalton, she taught school and waited.

The New England towns where David Lyman and Sarah Joiner grew up were steeped in an austere Calvinist tradition. Working on the Sabbath, card playing, smoking, gambling, immoderate drinking, and "frivolous behavior" were all earthly sins.

Long hours of hard work, thrift, self reliance, honesty, church attendance and home bible reading were virtues. The church was the focal point of their communities, and both the Lymans and Joiners were staunch church members.

As the eldest of ten, David worked around the farm and helped raise his siblings. His parents scrimped to send him to Williams College. David left college briefly to teach school, probably to earn money, then went back and graduated from Williams in 1828, and from the Andover Theological Seminary in 1831. He was ordained that same year and helped conduct evangelistic revival meetings throughout New England. In the summer of 1831, he visited Royalton, Vermont, where he was the houseguest of a local deacon named Salmon Joiner. He met Joiner's daughter Sarah, and the two found much in common.

David had volunteered for mission work and expected to work among the Indians in western New York State, but was instead selected by the ABCFM to join the Fifth Company leaving in a few weeks for Hawai'i. He had to get married at once, for the Board required that all male missionaries be accompanied by their wives. David then asked Sarah, who accepted.

They were married in a snowstorm in Royalton on November 2, 1831. The occasion was as much like a funeral as a wedding, with solemn men and weeping women sure that the young couple was going away forever. Their fears were realized—neither David nor Sarah ever left Hawai'i.

At 2AM, they climbed into the Royalton-Woodstock Transportation Company stagecoach and rumbled away in a blizzard, bound for Boston and then New Bedford, to board a ship fo r Hawai'i.

The Colonial-period spelling of "Mifsionary" was still being used when David received his ABCFM certificate. The document was signed by Rufus Anderson, the Mission's Foreign Secretary for whom the Lymans named their fifth son. Ten days after this document was issued to David, he and Sarah boarded the whaleship Averick *and headed half a world away, to their new life in the Sandwich Islands.*

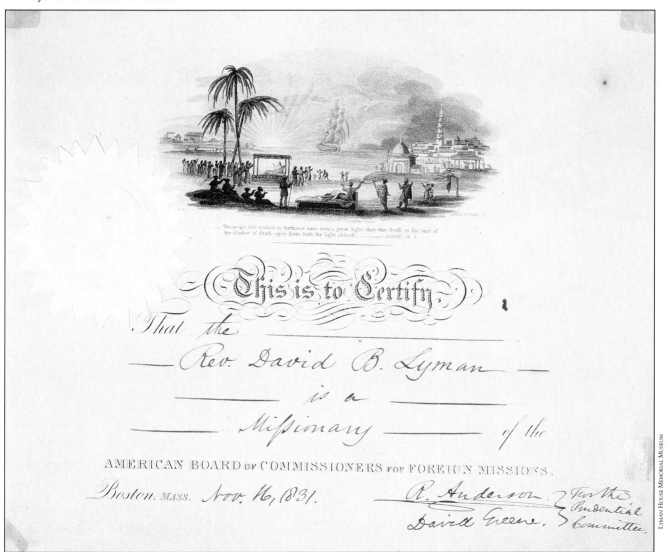

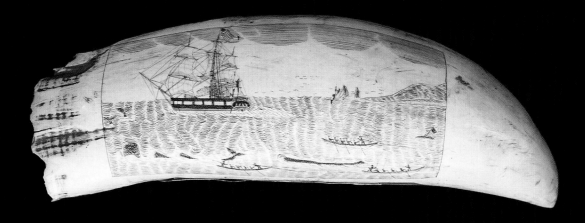

AVERICK

The ship which carried the Fifth Company of ABCFM
missionaries to the Islands had a history typical of a whaleship
of the day. Not three months before the Lymans had clambered
aboard, she had returned to New Bedford from her maiden Pacific
voyage, laden with 3150 barrels of sperm oil. For her 1831 voyage
with the missionaries, she was taken out by a new master, Edward
Swain, who died at Paita (on the coast of Peru) just a year after
dropping the Lymans in Honolulu. Eventually returning to New
Bedford, *Averick* made four more voyages, and in 1845, went
aground on the island of Raiatea. She was hauled off and ended
her days with a new name—*Recovery*—under the Chilean flag.

Voyage to the Sandwich Isles

It's now a simple matter to travel from Massachusetts to Hawai'i in less than half a day. But a century and a half ago, this same trip was a wretched one which took six months in a wallowing, pitching wooden sailing ship.

O n November 26, 1831, David and Sarah Lyman and the other young missionaries of the Fifth Company boarded the whaleship *Averick* at New Bedford, Massachusetts and set sail for the Sandwich Islands. This was a honeymoon voyage, as all nine couples had been married less than three months, but what a honeymoon it would be!

Years later, Henry Lyman described what his parents had told him of their departure: "It had been the intention of the commander to run down into the outer harbor, and, casting anchor there,

Facing page: This is the only existing original image of the whaleship Averick, *which carried the Lymans from New Bedford to Hawai'i. During the voyage, one of the crewmen scrimshawed the ship on this ivory sperm whale tooth. She is shown "port-painted," a widely-practiced technique of painting fake gunports along a white stripe on each side of the ship to frighten away ostensibly ferocious South Seas islanders.*

to complete his preparations for going to sea; for the ship was as yet far from being ready to leave port. But it was one of the most delightful days of Indian summer— so as the owner of the ship, who had accompanied the party down the bay, got into his boat to return to the city, he called to the Captain, 'Well, Swain, it's so pleasant I guess you better keep right on and run out to sea!'

"Very well, sir!" replied the officer, and crowding on all sail the good ship *Averick* was soon out of sight.

"The order of the ship owner proved to have been ill-considered. The deck was covered with sea stores that had been received at the last moment; the cabin was filled with coils of rope and misc-ellaneous articles thrown in from above to make room on the deck for more."

Averick was a sturdy, three-masted vessel, 110' long and 27' at her widest. She was specifically built to hunt whales and then render them into marketable products, not ferry passengers. On this trip, she not only had the 19-member Fifth Company crammed aboard, she also had supplies for the Hawai'i Mission.

David wrote his brother: "When we came on board Saturday morning we found our cabin literally three or four feet deep with boxes, trunks, etc. Steerage, (i.e. the large room forward of the cabin

OUTFIT FOR THE SANDWICH ISLANDS.

"Articles necessary as an outfit to the Sandwich Islands; it being deemed a sufficient supply for three years."

[Prepared by the Mission in 1834.]

Gentleman's Outfit for the Voyage, of 150 days.

1 sea cap and hat,
1 stock or black cravat,
25 old shirts,
25 collars,
2 vests, dark,
2 spencers, dark,
3 pr. pantaloons, dark,
14 pr. stockings,
2 pr. shoes,
1 cloak,
1 woollen suit,
5 pocket handkerchiefs,
11 changes of sheets,
21 towels,
3 lbs. soap,
2 flannel shirts,
10 pr. pillow cases,
2 blankets,
1 washbason, tin,
1 looking glass,
1 lamp.

—

Gentleman's Outfit for the Islands.

3 razors,
1 razor strap,
1 shaving box,
8 cakes shaving soap,
1 pocket compass,
1 good watch,
3 chrystals,
6 pocket handkerchiefs,
2 umbrellas,
1 fur hat,
15 shirts,
12 cravats,
18 collars,
8 vests,
12 pr. pantaloons, thin,
8 jackets, thin,
18 pr. stockings, thin,
2 pr. pantaloons, woollen,
1 jacket, do.
2 coats, do.
8 pr. stockings, do.
3 coats, thin,
6 pr. shoes, thick,
10 pr. do. thin,
3 pr. suspenders,
1 cloak,
2 black stocks,
4 pr. drawers,
2 flannel shirts.

Lady's Outfit for the Voyage.

1 hood,
1 sun-bonnet,
1 calash,
25 changes of linen, old,
4 petticoats, thin,
10 loose dresses, calico and gingham, dark and light,
1 loose double dress,
2 pr. stockings, woollen,
15 pr. do. thin,
1 cloak,
1 shawl,
3 pr. shoes,
2 black aprons,
15 night dresses,
1 fan.

—

Lady's Outfit for the Islands.

1 dress bonnet,
2 bonnets for common wear,
1 veil,
16 changes of linen or cotton,
12 dresses, calico or gingham,
1 dress, silk or crape,
2 dresses, thin, white, etc.
2 petticoats, flannel,
6 do. thin,
5 pr. stockings, woollen,
18 pr. do. thin,
8 neck handkerchiefs,
9 night dresses,
1 shawl, thick,
2 do. thin,
1 cloak,
4 pr. gloves,
10 pocket handkerchiefs,
1 parasol,
8 aprons,
6 pr. shoes, for walking,
6 pr. do. prunella, kid, morocco, etc.
2 combs, shell,
8 do. side,
2 fans,
shoe-strings, one piece,
ribbons,
1 bandbox, wooden,
10 yds. flannel,
10 yds. linen,
tapes, ferets, braids, pins, needles, threads of different kinds, hooks and eyes, pearl buttons, thimbles, etc.
3 pr. scissors,
1 pr. shears.

Furniture.

1 bookcase,
2 bedsteads,
1 table,
1 stand,
1 bureau,
2 looking-glasses,
12 chairs,
1 rocking chair,
2 writing desks, portable,
1 floor brush, hair,
2 brooms,
2 shoe brushes,
1 dusting brush and pan,
1 clothes brush,
1 clock, (price ten dollars,)
2 water buckets,
1 pr. bellows,
2 sieves,
1 nest Hingham boxes,
1 bread tray,
1 rolling pin,
24 clothes pins,
2 matresses, single,
4 pillows,
1 ticking, ready made,
3 bedquilts,
2 calico spreads,
3 blankets,
1 set bed curtains,
1 set mosquito curtains,
12 pr. sheets,
12 pr. pillow cases,
18 towels,
12 crash towels,
1 oil cloth,
5 table cloths, white,
25 yds. calico, for settees and window curtains,
30 yds. diaper,
6 table cloths, colored.

—

Crockery.

*12 teacups and saucers, (each,)
*6 coffee do. do.
*2 teapots,
*2 creamers,
2 sugar bowls,
8 bowls,
4 pitchers, different sizes,
4 mugs,
12 dining plates,

"* Not deemed necessary for ordinary purposes."

Facing page: The ABCFM prepared this list of "Articles necessary as an outfit to the Sandwich Islands; it being deemed a sufficient supply for three years." Above: A crowd turns out for the November, 1822 departure of Second Company missionaries leaving New Haven bound for Hawai'i. This scene is like that experienced by David and Sarah Lyman and the other members of the Fifth Company when they left New Bedford nine years later.

on each side of which are our rooms and through which we pass in going to them) filled in every part almost to the deck with articles of almost every description.

"I made it my first business to dig my way to my room and change my clothes, which I accomplished in the course of an hour, having injured the clothes I wore in no triffling degree by the paint and tar with which I came in contact along the way. It took until near night to get things a little arranged in our room."

And Sarah wrote her sister Melissa: "If you will just take the trouble to sleep in one of our closets at home with all the chamber windows closed, you can form some idea of the closeness of our rooms, our own room being just about the size of one of these closets. In that little room we have six trunks, a large bandbox, two book shelves, baskets, boxes, etc., besides clothing hung on nails."

Facilities in the cabin were no better: "When we embarked there were two

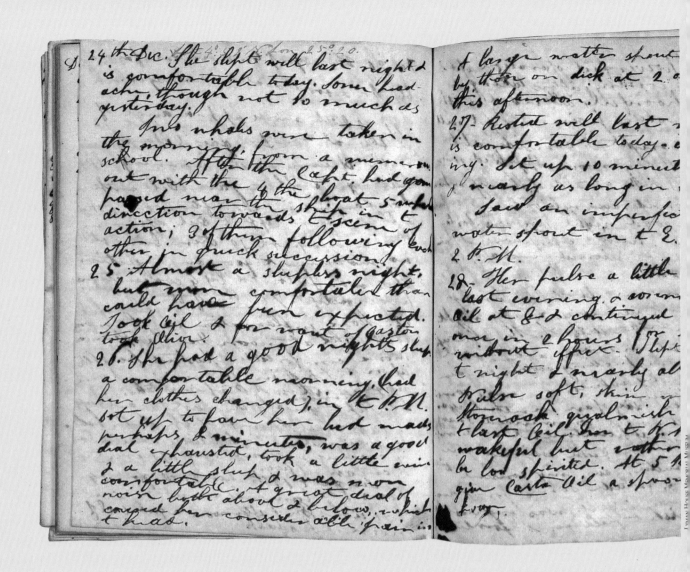

David's shipboard journal: *December 24:* [Sarah] "slept well last night and is comfortable today. Some headache though not so much as yesterday. Two whales were taken in the morning from a school."

On *December 25,* Sarah had "Almost a sleepless night, but more comfortable than could have been expected. Took Oil, for want of castor, took olive."

Note that David never mentions December 25th as Christmas, for these New Englanders did not celebrate the day whose very name, "Christ's Mass," reeked of Romanism and, by extension, the English Church. Early Colonial theologian Cotton Mather railed against celebrating what he called "wanton Bacchanalian Christmasses spent revelling, dicing, carding, masking, mumming, consumed in compotations, interludes, excesses of wine, in mad mirth..."

So eager were the Puritans to rid themselves of any hint of the Anglicanism that they passed laws prohibiting the celebration, which was not really accepted in New England until around the Civil War.

On *December 26,* Sarah is still resting and is quite weak: "She had a good night's sleep, a comfortable morning, (had her clothes changed) in the afternoon, sat up to have her bed made, perhaps 8 minutes, was a good deal exhausted, took a little wine and a little sleep, and was more comfortable. A great deal of noise, both above and below, which caused her considerable pain in the head."

The noise, undoubtedly, came from the whalers, busy processing their catch. Whaling was hard, dirty, dangerous work. Once a whale was captured, the process shifted to "trying out" or rendering the carcass into marketable products. Blankets of blubber had to be peeled off the floating whale, then winched aboard and cut into successively smaller pieces to be melted in the huge iron trypots. The resulting oil was cooled, put in casks and crammed into every nook and cranny of the hold in the very belly of the ship. The shouts of the men, the roar of the tryworks fires, the pounding of the cooper up on deck making casks and the rumble of barrels rolling and the grunts of the men rolling them, all were more than enough to give Sarah a headache.

chairs for the use of the officers and our whole company. One of these has since broken." Those who could eat, stood or sat on chests, kegs, barrels. There wasn't room for everyone, so there were two mess calls. A couple shared a plate, cup, bowl and tableware. Frequently the ship rolled and pitched so much it was impossible to keep dishes on the table despite its raised rim.

The ship was still a shambles when— less than a day out of port—a storm blew up. David wrote: "Morning found 18 out of 19 of our number seasick. The storm continued and all were obliged to keep their berths nearly the whole time. Of course the Sabbath passed without any public religious exercises. On Monday and Tuesday the storm increased so that we were obliged to lie (i.e. to furl the sails, turn the ship's head to the wind, and let her drift). This we did one day to prevent being driven on the coast by contrary winds, and on another because it was impossible either to get the boats in, or to proceed without destroying them if left in their usual position."

Crates of live poultry, vegetables and other cargo on deck were washed away, along with a cask of oil for the ship's lamps. Only a pint could be salvaged from a second cask to light the one lamp used to aid in steering the ship at night.

A tub of butter and a bucket of tar wedged at the foot of the stairs leading to the cabin. Coming down the steps, the first mate stepped first in one and then the other, cursing and shaking his fists. The missionaries burned butter to give a little light in the dark interior of the ship, likely from this same tub.

The storm lulled, then brewed into a hurricane, described by David: "The ship was several times thrown upon her beam ends (i.e. thrown over upon her side so as to bring her railing under the water and lay the masts down touching the waves). At one time they were upon the point of cutting away the foremast. Frequently, for two or three days the waves dashed over us and some were obliged to abandon their rooms on account of it."

Despite damage, *Averick* stayed afloat, but others caught in the storm were not so lucky. Betsey Lyons' journal: "The

LAHAINA WHALING MUSEUM

wreck passed us. Everything and every person had probably been swept from the deck. Nothing was left standing but a solitary mast. Ropes and sails were dragging after the ship, in the water."

As the storm howled, Sarah became seasick and developed a high fever. The Fifth Company physician, Dr. Alonzo Chapin, "Bled her copiously and as this did not produce all the effect he desired, he repeated it in a few hours. On the 22nd of December she was again bled and gained uniformally from that time."

A typical whaling scene, repeated a number of times on the Averick as the Fifth Company missionaries sailed towards the Islands. The whalers have dropped their small boats into the ocean, and are attacking a large sperm whale.

Bloodletting—or phlebotomy—was a standard medical procedure of the time. It was practiced by both doctors and barbers (whose traditional red and white pole reflects the practice). Leeches were often used, though Dr. Chapin used a scalpel. Bloodletting was thought to relieve pressure and dilute infections by reducing the blood supply. It was a risky practice— some 32 years before, George Washington died after being bled for what is now thought to have been strep throat.

Sarah was lucky to have survived both "the billious fever which brought me to the borders of the grave" and the treatment, an early indication of her mettle, for she lived to reach eighty.

Like Sarah, the *Averick* weathered the storm. Edward Swain was a capable master, and the missionaries spoke of his kindnesses, his attendance at their services "though not a religious man" and his skill at handling ship and crew.

Sarah was not nearly so impressed with the rowdy whalers: "A more wicked set of men I presume could not have been collected together than our crew are. I never in my whole life heard so much profanity, as since I came on board..."

The hurricane had driven them off course into the Sargasso Sea, a patch of ocean called the "swamp," where they were becalmed for a time.

Averick was, of course, first and foremost a whaleship, her passengers incidental, and the cry of "Thar she blows!" galvanized the crew. Whaleboats dropped in pursuit of the Leviathan, and a successful hunt turned the ship into a factory, with blubber boiled into oil in the smoky trypots amidships.

On January 11, after 57 days at sea, *Averick* put in at Rio de Janeiro to repair a damaged mast and to take on supplies. Fortunately for Sarah, who was "unable to walk without assistance," they stayed almost a month, as houseguests of an English couple. There they reveled in fresh milk, fruit and vegetables. After extensive repairs, the ship left Rio for the trip around the dreaded Cape Horn—a passage that was remarkably uneventful.

Sarah again became ill, again was bled and remained weak for the rest of the voyage. *Averick* cruised towards the Islands, whaling as the occasion arose. There were no more storms, but the heat near the equator was both overpowering and inescapable, on deck or below. The Company passed the time with laundry, mending, sewing—and in study. Sarah, oddly, brushed up on Greek. There were religious services, hymn singing, endless discussions and exercise. Skipping rope was a favorite, as was walking the deck.

Averick planned to return to New England in a few months, so letters were given to Captain Swain to mail there. At last they caught sight of Maui, then Moloka'i and O'ahu, where they dropped anchor in Honolulu Harbor on May 17, 1832. The voyage had taken 173 days—almost six months.

Hawaiians paddled out to the ship in canoes laden with fresh fruits and other missionaries—in Honolulu for their annual General Meeting—who came aboard to greet them. Some of the women, including Sarah, were too weak to walk far, and Ka'ahumanu sent a royal carriage to take them to the home of Rev. Hiram Bingham, self-proclaimed leader of the Sandwich Islands Mission.

David and Sarah stayed in Honolulu almost two months before going to Hilo. They learned much about the Hawaiians, their customs, language and traditions.

Honolulu had more contact—both good and bad—with people from other lands. Superficially, at least, it seemed more "civilized," with some frame and stone buildings and shops. A number of foreigners lived there, and many of the Hawaiians spoke English, and wore Western-style clothes.

While the Lymans were in Honolulu, Ka'ahumanu died after a long illness. She had been Kamehameha's favorite wife and was the most powerful woman—person, really—in the Kingdom. She was also a zealous convert who had been a great help to the missionaries. Since the death of Kamehameha in 1819 (and Kamehameha II in 1825), she had served as *kuhina nui* (regent). David and Sarah attended her elaborate state funeral.

On July 5, 1832 the Lymans set sail on the *Waverly* for their Mission in Hilo. On the way, they were becalmed, spent almost three days in Lahaina, battled stiff winds in the 'Alenuihāhā Channel and tore a sail. They detoured to Kawaihae, where they were guests of John Young, the oldest *haole* in the Islands, and a long-time advisor to Kamehameha I. The rough weather over, they left for Hilo.

On July 16, *Waverly* dropped anchor in Hilo Bay, and sent passengers and cargo ashore in small boats. David and Sarah Lyman were "home" at last.

The Lymans Arrive in Hilo

"The scenery was wild and romantic. The breadfruit tree with wide spreading branches and bright glossy leaves, was scattered in rich profusion and flowers in great abundance; the morning glory entwined itself around the trunks of the stately trees and found its way to their verry tops, giving them a singularly romantic appearance."

Sarah Joiner Lyman, August 31, 1832

Hawai'i Island is—and isn't—a tropical paradise. For it is a continent in miniature, both hot and cold, wet and dry. There are snow-capped peaks, molten and hardened lava, desolate shimmering deserts spiked with cactus, lush rolling hills dotted with cattle, beaches of white, green and black sand, and dense rain forests.

Hilo is a very green, very wet place. Warm tropic air sweeping in from the sea collides with 13,677' Mauna Loa and dumps some 140" of rain on Hilo each year. The area is a magnet for nature's primal forces. Rolling earthquakes, huge

tsunamis and the ever-present threat of an advancing wall of molten rock—all were a part of the Lyman's life in Hilo, just as they are a part of life in Hilo today.

Rev. Hiram Bingham had toured the Island just two years before the Lymans' arrived: "I was struck with the grandeur, extent, and the beauty of the scenery presented to the eye by Hawaii. Here appeared the smooth bay of Hilo and its ample beach sweeping round in graceful curvature, skirted with hamlets and cottages amounting to three or four hundred habitations, verdant banks, shrubbery, and a variety of trees—the tall valuable and uncivilized cocoanut, and the shady, noble, useful breadfruit. Among the scattered trees rose the humble yet capacious thatched church, just dedicated to almighty God for the use of the thousands of the population of Hilo and Puna districts and near it the shapely 2-story decently furnished mission house, painted white, with its neat little portico and raised panel koa door, furnishing a slight specimen of civilization and symbol of domestic comfort amidst the richness and roughness of Hawaiian foliage.

"There the more frail and widely scattered dwellings of the farmer and fisherman were seen, some just raising their dingy tops about the foliage of

Facing page: Sarah was especially impressed by the breadfruit tree, with its fat, edible fruit and enormous tropical leaves.

Hilo in 1825. This image shows early thatched missionary homes occupied by the Goodrich and Ruggles families next to the Waiākea River on Hilo Bay. When the Lymans arrived seven years later, the Mission had moved to safer ground uphill. This drawing is by Robert Dampier, an artist aboard the British frigate H.M.S. Blonde, which sailed to the Islands to return the bodies of Kamehameha II and his wife Kamāmalu, who had both died of measles in London while on a royal visit.

bananas, sugar cane, and shrubs, and some in bold relief, standing upon a green bank or mound, and other shaded by a tree or group of trees."

Native homes had thatched roofs. The walls—if there were walls—were thatched as well, with no windows and just a low doorway. Floors were packed earth, strewn with grass or with mats laid over them. Some had raised stone floors with a top dressing of small waterworn pebbles called 'ili'ili. There was no wharf in Hilo in those days, no shops, roads or bridges. Life was quieter, more primitive and less affected by traders, whalers and missionaries than Honolulu or Lahaina.

The Hilo Mission had been founded six years earlier, in 1824, by Rev. Joseph Goodrich and Samuel Ruggles. The two families manned it, but on an almost occasional basis: Goodrich from 1824-6 and 1830-2 and Ruggles from 1824-5 and 1826-8. When the Lymans got to Hilo in 1832, the Goodriches were in residence, as were the Jonathan Greens.

The Lymans shared a thatched house with the Greens—who were about to depart for Maui, in hopes of improving their health. A hanging mat divided one room into two, and after storing all their trunks and boxes, there was scarcely more space than David and Sarah had had aboard *Averick*. After the Greens left, Rev. and Mrs. Sheldon Dibble took their places in the cramped house.

David took Rev. Dibble on a tour of churches and schools along the wet, Hāmākua Coast. Drenched by teeming rain, they crossed turbulent streams and clambered up and down steep gulches.

David: "...It had rained considerably during the previous night and the morning was wet. The first hour and one-fourth of the walk [from Hilo to Hakalau] the streams were but little swollen. We then came to one so much enlarged that the native with us endeavored to persuade us to return, but we concluded to ford it, which we did, finding it about waist high in the center. The next stream was so swollen that we hesitated whether to attempt crossing it. The water was deep and rapid and neither of us could swim. At length a rope was obtained and we pulled ourselves across by it...We found but three more in which the water was deep. Two of these we forded and the third we swam by means of the rope."

Natural History of Man.

Inhabitants of the Sandwich Islands

A Hawaiian couple appears in this hand-colored aquatint from an early 1840s edition of Dr. Prichard's Natural History of Man, *published in London.*

37

He popoki huhu.　　He ilio hae.

E na pokii; e akahi; e akahele;
mai hailiili; mai kuamuamu; mai ha-
kaka me ka inaina; mai nuku aku
kekahi i kekahi; e waiho i na hua
hilahila.

Mai huhu hala ole aku ia hai. Ua
huhu hala ole o Kaina i kona kaikaina
ia Abela, a pepehi iho la ia ia.

Mai hoomaewaewa iki aku. Ua
hoomaewaewa kekahi poe kamalii i
ke kaula maikai ia Elisai, a ua make
lakou i na holoholona hihiu hae; ka-
nahakumamalua ka i make.

I mai la Iesu, Ua hoopuni mai na
ilio ia'u; ua o mai lakou i ko'u mau
lima, a me ko'u mau wawae.

I mai la Solomona, Me ka ilio i hoi
hou ai i kona luai, pela ke kanaka
hewa i hoi hou ai i kona hewa.

He keko apiki.　　He puaa uhauha.

Mai manao nui ma ke kino, ma ka
mea e lealea ai. Mai ona lama. No
ka naaupo a me ka naau ino ka ono
lama. He mea ia e make ai.

E ala oukou e na mea ona lama, e
uwe hoi, e auwe aku hoi oukou e na
mea ona waina.

I mai la Petero. O ka mea i lohe i
ka olelo a ke Akua a haalele i ka ino
o ke ao nei, a hoi hou aku ma ka hewa, ua like no ia me ka puaa i holoiia
a hoi hou no i kona moe ana i ka lepo.
2*

Pages from a learning-to-read primer called Buke Mua Hua *(First Book of Letters) showing a huhū (angry) cat and a monkey drinking something from an unusually-shaped glass.*

On the way home, David described the conditions: "...the Wailuku was so swollen as to render it impossible to cross at the usual place. Being told by the natives that it was good crossing in canoes at its mouth, we went thither. It was then about 8 and quite dark. Our clothes were dripping and we must either sleep in them as they were or get home.

"So far as we could judge in the dark, the place was such a one as we wished. Accordingly we seated ourselves in a canoe and pushed off. At first we glided along quietly, but when we came where the current of the river came down with all its strength on one side and the surf beat heavily upon us from the other, the canoe was repeatedly thrown almost out of the water. Once the outrigger flew up to a considerable height and probably would have gone over...had there not been a number of natives in the canoe who were skillful in managing it. As it was we reached the shore in safety with our canoe about half filled with water..."

In contrast, trips to the dry Puna district to inspect schools and conduct services were difficult in other ways, for they had to trudge miles over rough lava and through tangled forests. Settlements were small, although hundreds often gathered when they stopped to preach.

Even in sleepy Hilo, Hawaiian society could not escape the weight of traders who exchanged foreign goods for local resources. The ancient economic system was collapsing, as the Hawaiians' communal sense of land management and aquaculture collided with the capitalist individualism of whalers and merchants.

As the age-old *kapu* faded, and the Hawaiian class system lost its meaning, the Lymans saw education as an urgent task that required transplanting not only Christianity, but the essential survival skills of their New England culture.

In Hawaiian tradition, children had learned from their parents, grandparents and extended families. Now they faced hours in a classroom, learning the alphabet from kind but insistent strangers. If life for centuries had focused on the present, it now turned toward the future, toward what was necessary to earn a daily living and more importantly, an eternity in heaven.

Like their predecessors, David and Sarah rapidly learned Hawaiian and used it to teach, and David's journals and letters are sprinkled with Hawaiian words and phrases. They realized that to bring Christianity to those they saw in need, they had to adopt pieces of island culture themselves. Yet they firmly believed that if the community were to flourish, Hawaiians needed the practical skills of New England. The culture forged by these changes inevitably would be a hybrid, one in which both groups would struggle to keep what they valued most.

By the time the Lymans had arrived at Hilo Mission, Hawaiian had been given written form by earlier missionaries,

who reduced it phonetically, first to seventeen letters and then to twelve.

Sarah began to "examine" schools the day after she got to Hilo. Many pupils were still in the alphabet and primer stage of reading. These people knew almost nothing about written language before coming to school, but they knew that traders, foreign settlers, high chiefs, their king and queen, and the missionaries all set a great deal of importance to the small marks made on paper, the *palapala*.

The first thing Hawaiians learned was the alphabet, which they called *pīāpā* from the way they were taught to say "b a ba, c a ca" to learn the sounds and shapes of these letters. They also learned to write letters on slates or paper, or if these were not available, on big leaves or wet sand.

School lasted only a few hours each day, but not many came every day, for a routine of that nature was alien to the Hawaiians. They were, however, fearful of disobeying Ka'ahumanu's edict that they learn to read and write and attend Sunday church services.

Most of the early pupils were adult *ali'i* (chiefs), but later, schools primarily taught children. A week after her arrival, Sarah wrote: "I this day commenced my writing school. Those who attended are teachers, have written some before, though they have devoted little time to it...I enjoy it pretty well but am exceedingly tired in consequence of not being able to talk with them."

On September 5, 1832, she noted: "The schools in this region to the number of thirty (some of them numbering from sixty to eighty schollar) met in the church and passed examination. The school that I have the superintendence of numbers 100 schollars, all, with two or three exceptions, drest in black tapa gowns and straw hats of their own manufacture with wreaths of flowers around their necks." The outlying schools had native teachers, for so many were needed that as fast as a student (some only fourteen years old) was proficient, he began teaching others. Later, many were put in charge of their own schools, which gave them status albeit very little pay.

Wherever possible there were at least two teachers to a school, one to stay and teach while the other went to Hilo for additional training. Then they changed places. All the missionaries at Hilo helped train teachers.

"213 Makoa"

Artist Dampier noted: "They are fond of tattooing...Cows, Goats, and other animals on their foreheads and cheeks." The missionaries railed hard against this practice.

Lofty ideals rooted in Aristotle and Calvin were taught in quarters Sarah found extremely primitive yet functional: "The school house is delightfully situated in a grove of cocoanut trees, but I was truly disgusted with the scene presented within. In one end were calabashes, baskets, and fishing utensils, and a place to bake food. In that end in which the school was kept there was neither bench nor mat. The ground was covered with dead grass which gave it a stable-like appearance. On this the teachers and schollars seated themselves after having procured a mat for me...I was on the whole well pleased with the school as it was managed so much better than native schools in general are."

In addition to reading and writing, Sarah taught history, arithmetic, geography—and a sewing class so Hawaiian women could make "modest" garments to cover themselves from neck to ankle. These were first made from *kapa* bark-cloth, sewn with *olonā* thread.

She discouraged any leis or flowers in women's hair, and instead taught the making of hats, which became a brief fashion rage. As the novelty wore off, Sarah noted sadly that women carried their hats until they neared church, donned them for services, and removed them again after they'd gone a short ways.

Music has always been part of Island life. The Hawaiians had a long history of chanting, but that was discouraged by the missionaries because of its ties to 'pagan' religion and their traditional culture. Missionaries especially frowned on the ribald songs of drunken sailors and even on secular songs of the day. The Lymans'

These silhouettes, done about 1848 before photography was readily available in the Islands, are the earliest known images of David and Sarah. They were made by Persis Thurston Taylor, who was both an ABCFM daughter (Asa and Lucy Thurston) and wife (Rev. T.E. Taylor). She traced their shadows and then cut them out of dark paper.

preference, of course, was hymns, and they set up an extremely popular singing school. Hawaiians delighted in the rich harmonies, and the Lymans would rejoice to hear today's Haili Church choir, famous for their hymns sung in Hawaiian.

By 1832, the printing presses at Honolulu and Lahainaluna were turning out primers, spellers, arithmetic books, catechisms, Bible tracts, most of the New Testament, even a periodical of sorts. But demand still far outstripped supply, and many schools suffered a lack of new reading material while presses suffered from a lack of paper and supplies. In these early days, David supervised outlying schools, advising new teachers.

He also distributed and sold books and tracts written in Hawaiian, taking payment in food, *kapa*, or labor around the Mission. In his journal, David notes: "Our examination of schools...occupied Monday and Tuesday, since which I have sold about 600 books, and almost written one sermon, though I fear it will hardly be fit to preach."

Not content with Hawaiians merely learning by rote, David wrote: "I had a third meeting for the people living near and questioned them on my sermons. Three or four had used slates and were prepared not only to name the texts and heads of the sermons but had retained most of the principal thoughts and cited

He'e nalu *(surfing) was uniquely Hawaiian, and frowned upon by the missionaries as a prodigious waste of time, among other things. Sarah writes: "You have probably heard that playing on the surf board was a favourite amusement in ancient times. It is too much practised at the present day, and is the source of much iniquity, inasmuch as it leads to intercourse with the sexes without discrimination. Today a man died on his surf board. He was seen to fall from it, but has not yet been found. I hope this will be a warning to others, and that many will be induced to leave this foolish amusement."*

most of the texts quoted in their support."

In early years, when chiefs still had control, David could complain about poor attendance, and have the district chief order his people—and sometimes the teacher—back to school. Sarah tells of going through the neighborhood to round up pupils and admonish their parents. She finally limited herself to a "select school" of pupils nearby so she wouldn't have to travel so far to hunt up truants.

David's problems took a different twist: "I heard this evening that a worker of wickedness has gone out from this place to Puna, that multitudes of people have gone after him, and that some of them have brought their books to their teacher saying they wanted nothing more of the word of God or of schools. This is only another evidence that we are yet among a heathen people."

The Lymans seldom used the rod, meting out discipline in other ways. Sarah: "A boy perhaps 10 years of age, made so much disturbance that I was obliged to separate him from his class; at the close of the school I prohibited his marching with us, took him home with me where I kept him tied two or three hours., I then, after talking with him, sent him home. The next morning he did not appear in the school room. I sent for him, but as soon as he saw the individual approaching he ran off and could not be found till night. Monday morning Barenaba led him to school. He appeared quite humble and since has been a good boy, has worked in the garden this week and procured two new books. The course which I pursued with him had a good effect on the other schollars."

Lessons usually lasted two or three hours, then class was dismissed. Sarah describes her working day: "Night finds me exhausted with the fatigues of the day. From 8 (am) till half past 10, I was in the cook house giving lessons to my new cook. I find it exceedingly trying to teach new help; but I flatter myself that when he is learnt he will do my work more agreeably to my wishes than one who has been employed by others.

"This pm I have spent wholly with the natives. At 12 my schollars came as usual to work on their maps. They left at 2, and 10 females came to line and bind the maps and prepare them for examination at 4. I went into my school where I remained till tea time. Very soon after tea the bell rang for singing school, from which I have just returned, and now at half past eight I have 9 natives at work in the adjoining room, some writing, some drawing maps, and some sewing."

Reading and writing skills took precedence in the schools—especially outlying ones with native teachers—and literacy flourished in the Kingdom. By 1832, half the adult population could read, a record better than many European nations of the day, and even more remarkable because Hawaiians had no written language in 1820.

Both Sarah and David and other missionaries bemoaned the slowness of Hawaiians to adopt their "civilized" ways and Christian morality. Their journals lament that "the people go on to sin" by maintaining their old ways—knocking out their front teeth as a sign of grief, tattooing themselves, dancing the hula, wailing and chanting, surfing"—as well as sins of a more Ten Commandment bent: stealing, lying, adultery and gambling.

On visits to native homes, Sarah carried her "tobacco roll book" listing those who smoked, plus those who quit, and of course, backsliders. Smoking, drunkenness and adultery were serious enough offenses to warrant excommunication. The more penitent sinners were later readmitted to church.

A few months after their arrival in Hilo, the Lymans were given a new thatched home built by the Hawaiians "for aloha." On October 24, 1832, Sarah wrote in her journal: "This is a day long to be remembered, as it witnessed us inmates of our own dwelling. We moved hither today, and this evening our table was spread for the first time since our marriage. Our house is new and neatly finished for a native house, and is delightfully situated fronting the sea. The natives called to congratulate us."

On the same day, David, always dutiful, showed his frustration: "It has cost me considerable time and a good deal of thought and vexation to prepare [the new house] so that it should be comfortable. I have now no study table, no inside doors, and am destitute of many other things equally necessary to render us comfortable and to enable us to prosecute our work with success..."

David's journal notes his guilt about the intrusions of ordinary chores, time he felt he should be studying, praying, or writing/re-writing sermons. Always a perfectionist, he worked hard to use exactly the right Hawaiian phrases, difficult in a language which had almost infinitely subtle shades of meaning.

Sarah understood his need for perfection and wrote her sister: "One thing I forgot to mention in mother's letter, and that is, to request her to bring up her daughters, now under her care, to be more particular than I am, for I am not half enough so, to please my husband. I used to think myself quite a neat girl, but have about come to the conclusion that I am far from being so. It will not do for me to have one hair out of place, or a speck of dirt on my frock or apron."

Sarah concentrated on missionary work while her Hawaiian domestics did the household chores. Missionary wives—Sarah included—kept a New England home, as best they could, for they were convinced that nothing but their own traditions could conceivably be correct. They wore clothing not remotely suited to the climate and preferred—when they could get it—food imported round the Horn: flour, butter, cheese and dried apples. They persisted even though these foodstuffs might arrive moldy, insect infested, exposed to rats and mice, or soaked by sea water. At the time, no one realized what bacteria was, much less that it could be harmful, and most of the missionaries were frequently ill.

The Goodrichs had planted taro, bananas, grapes and squash, and the Hawaiians often made gifts of poi, fish, chickens or pork. The missionaries could buy fresh or smoked beef that hunters brought down from the mountains. Still, their diet was often rudimentary. Sarah wrote: "No eggs, no fish and no melons. We are destitute of both fish and pork for the school, and have over 60 boys. We made our supper tonight (as we not infrequently do) entirely of taro. We have it fried in the morning, toasted at noon, and roasted at night."

The Lymans traded for most things they needed. Surplus went to other missions or to headquarters in Honolulu, where it was credited to their account. The island missions were run semi-communally. The ABCFM sent money

and goods to Honolulu, where Rev. Levi Chamberlain kept the commissary. A missionary's salary was credited to him there and items ordered were charged to his account or that of his Mission. Very little cash was involved.

The chief item for barter was cloth, which the Lymans then exchanged for firewood, lumber, wages of domestic help, even teachers' salaries. Cumbersome as it was, the system worked, though David was irked by frequent mistakes, long delays, missing items and time consumed by tiny details.

In the early days in Hilo, David spent more of his energy preaching and making converts than teaching people to read and write. He was discouraged by an inability to turn Hawaiians from "sinful" ways, and he also missed the fervor he remembered from New England revivals. More and more missionary burdens fell on the Lymans, as the Dibbles grew sicker and went to Maui, leaving the Goodrichs, soon to return to the U.S. at the behest of the Board, after he had almost left the Mission to manage Kōloa Plantation.

At the 1835 General Meeting, Rev. and Mrs. Titus Coan were assigned to Hilo, at the request of the Lymans and probably also because Hiram Bingham saw a threat from this dynamic, spell-binding preacher. Given Bingham's ferocious defense of his "authority," it is little surprise that Coan was sent as far away from Honolulu as possible, to the most remote Mission in the Islands. For five months, the Lymans shared the tiny stone house with the Coans, until the Goodrichs left, and the Coans moved into the frame house.

THE MOUNTAIN MAUNA KEA FROM HILO.

Outlines quite false; insolently exaggerated T,M

Isabella Bird was an English spinster who visited the Islands in 1873 and wrote a book, Six Months in the Sandwich Islands. *She calls Hilo "the paradise of Hawaii" and David Lyman (then 70) "very old and frail, the indefatigable head of an industrial school for native young men." One reader scrawled this irate note about Mauna Kea's Alp-like illustration.*

Titus Coan quickly mastered the Hawaiian tongue, thanks to the Lymans and Blind Bartemius, an early native convert. He was soon preaching in Hawaiian with the same power he had in English. During his first year, he circled the island, and "On this first tour, occupying 30 days, he nearly suffered shipwreck, or rather canoe-wreck, as also twice afterward. He preached 43 times in 8 days, ten of them in two days, examined 20 schools and more than 1200 scholars, conversed personally with multitudes, and ministered to many sick persons, for he was in a mild way a physician."

A new frame house for the Lymans and a larger school house was being built

as Sarah was in the last months of her second pregnancy. On November 26, 1835, Henry Munson Lyman was born and two months later, the Lymans and their sons moved into their new home. Sarah loved its dryness and roominess. There was no kitchen—cooking was out back in a stone oven—but a guest room was "fitted with a bedstead, chairs, and a washing establishment for the accomodation of the stranger whom Providence may direct to these distant shores."

Hilo had no hotels in 1836—nor for a long time thereafter—and the Lymans hosted hundreds, perhaps thousands, of visitors over the years. David Douglas, the Scottish botanist who lost his life on

Mauna Kea, stayed with them, as did Lt. Charles Wilkes of the U.S. Exploring Expedition, and many notable Hawaiians.

Their furnishings were simple and plain. Some were home-made, others came with them aboard *Averick*. Henry Lyman: "Every article was of the cheapest and plainest description, though some of the woodwork sawed out of the beautiful Hawaiian *koa*, might have been very ornamental had it been polished. There were a large arm-chair for my father, a rocking chair for my mother, a high-chair for the baby, and a lot of red painted

Fidelia and the Rev. Titus Coan, in a daguerreotype taken about 1850.

kitchen chairs. No carpets of any kind covered the floors, no paper the plastered walls, no blinds were at the windows, only some plain white cotton sash-curtains. The sole decoration consisted of a looking glass with a gilded frame that hung in the dining room, and a few coarsely colored lithographic cards, representing incidents in the life of Jesus, suspended on the walls in the bedrooms."

At long last, David and Sarah had their own room. The children stayed in during the day, or played outside in a walled enclosure behind the house, for early missionaries tried to cloister their children from Hawaiians, lest they learn 'heathen ways.' Reports from Tahiti—where earlier missionaries' children mingled freely with Tahitians—advised that such children grew up more native than American in culture and religion.

Sarah notes: "There are now many strangers here from...Puna, men, women, and children. Some converse with us on the all important subject [religion], but most crowd around our houses from idle curiosity and are very troublesome. We are obliged to confine them to one room, for if permitted to go where they please, our house would be thronged in every part of it from morning till night."

As David worked with outlying schools, he became more convinced of the need for a boarding school where select students would be under missionary supervision twenty-four hours a day, preparing to go forth as Christian pastors, teachers and leaders of the Kingdom.

In late May 1836, the Lymans and Coans sailed from Hilo to Lahaina and on to Honolulu, for the annual General

Meeting, the big social, religious and business event of the year. For the more remote missionaries, especially, it was a chance to compare ideas and shop at the Station House and stores of Honolulu.

Sarah penned in her journal that "sixteen sons and daughters have been born to our reinforcement. Three of the sons have died." It was an ominous observation, for a few days later, two-year-old David fell ill with *cholera infantum*. He died after several days of high fever and was buried in Lahaina on the way home.

Sarah wrote of their homecoming in Hilo: "The children and many of the people were assembled at the landing place to meet us and when we landed we found them all in tears; for they had not heard the afflictive intelligence till after our vessel anchored. Chairs were brought for us and we all set down and wept together. We then sang a hymn and Mr. L. prayed. Mrs. Coan [who was far advanced in pregnancy] and myself were so much debilitated we could not walk, and were carried to our dwellings... As I went into my room ...where're I turned my eye, I saw something to remind me of the dear departed boy. Desolation reigns in our once cheerful home."

Though the 1836 General Meeting marked the death of their son, another development there changed the Lymans, and Hilo, forever. At David's request, a boarding school for Hawaiian boys was authorized. Sarah noted that her husband and Titus Coan—of such different personalities and talents—divided their duties: "On returning home...it was decided that, as Mr. Coan was not particularly fond of teaching, and Mr.

Many missionaries were extremely interested in the Islands' flora and fauna. Fidelia Coan painted a series of native Hawaiian birds.

Lyman had had considerable experience in that line, he take the school."

From then on, Titus Coan did most of the preaching, and David Lyman handled the day-to-day administration of the Mission, started Hilo Boarding School and took over responsibility for other schools around Hilo. The division worked perfectly. David disliked trudging around the island preaching, but had expertise teaching. Coan saw each trip, no matter how arduous, as an adventure, and his restless nature chafed with the routine of teaching school.

While Coan was busy ministering, David was busy building Hilo Boarding School. He supervised construction of its first building and taught the boys who arrived before it was finished.

	Name.	Entered.	Rec'd, the Church.	Remarks.
1839.-40.	*Hilo*			
No. 75.	Kahumoku.	Oct. 1839.		Dis. 1844 ✳ 1853.
" 76.	" Paele	"		Mis. Sem. /41 ✳
" 77.	" Josepa	"		teacher, taylor &. Dis. 1849 ✳ 1866.
" 78.	" Kauwealoha.	"		visitor, + Mis'y Marquesas Mis Sem. 1840.
	Kohala.			
" 79.	Naiapaakai	Jan. 1840		Judge &c. Mis Sem. 1840 ✳
	Hilo			
" 80.	Peniamina	"		Ex. 1849 ✳ 1857. taylor
	Maui			
" 81.	Enoka.	Oct. 1839.		Mis. Sem. ✳ 186-
	Hilo			
" +82.	Sila	"		Mis. Sem. 1841.
" 83.	" Auwepaa	"		Dis. 1840. ✳ 1845
1840.-41.	N. Kona. *School year commenced with 59 scholars ended with 55.*			
" 84.	Hanakahialii	July 1840		Mis. Sem. 1841. ✳ /'45.
" 85.	" Heleloa	"		Dis. 1844.
" 86.	" Kanakaole	"		Mis. Sem. 1843.

Hilo Boarding School The Early Years

Every educational endeavor attempts to link the values of the past with the hopes for the future. With the advent of a boarding school, Hawaiian culture in Hilo took one more step toward the values of the New England life that the missionaries had left behind. In the inevitable struggle each school faces between the freedom of those it serves and a need for order, HBS struck the balance firmly but kindly toward order.

Hilo Boarding School officially opened on Monday, October 3, 1836, and a week later David noted: "Received the eight scholars to the school. Have prayers at 20 minutes past 5 am. Breakfast at 15 minutes past 6. Labor from 7 to 9, then bathe and study in Geography till lunch. Dine at 15 minutes

Facing page: HBS Student Register for the 1839-40 school year. The 75th student to enroll since the school opened three years earlier was a young man named Kahumoku from Hilo. Ironically, none of the boys were "Rec'd Church," although the Great Revival was in full swing. Right: A silhouette of Frederick Swartz Lyman, about 1848.

past 12. At half past 1 read the Natural History of Beasts till 2. Then study Helu Kamalii (arithmetic) till 3:30, then recite. At four and one half labor one hour. Supper at 6. Prayers at 7."

Sarah, in mid-November: "The boys have today planted rows of pineapples each side of the walk leading to Mr. Coan's...I now spend my afternoons in the schoolroom. Write with the boys after dinner, sit by them when they get their lessons, keep them in order while our native assistant hears them in arithmetic, and render him what assistance he needs. I shall also instruct them in singing. They have commenced learning the rules."

In December, Sarah wrote: "Since we commenced our school we have found but little trouble in obtaining a supply of food for the boys, though we have been obliged to give a higher price than usual on account of the scarcity. This week we found ourselves destitute, and those who had it for sale asked such an exorbitant price we could not feel justified in purchasing. So instead of sending the boys to pull taro on Thursday night (preceding their baking day), we sent them up into the trees for breadfruit. This they made into poi but of an inferior kind...Today a canoe arrived...bringing 15 bundles of hard poi...to pay for books. Thus the Lord takes care of us."

HILO, HAWAII.

Above: This pencil sketch was made by Edward Bailey in 1838 and shows HBS in its earliest days. Bailey was a multi-talented missionary, who designed churches, mills, roads and bridges in the Islands. He was also a gifted musician, poet, naturalist, amateur physician and teacher.

From the very first, the curriculum of HBS stressed good work habits and good citizenship as much as reading, writing, arithmetic and religion. Not everyone lasted. Homesickness claimed a few victims, including a seven-year-old who dropped out. Some students never even enrolled after their parents demanded payment in taro, tapa or cloth for giving up their sons to the school.

Sarah, Fidelia Coan and native women sewed durable blue cotton shirts and pants for the students, some of whom arrived wearing *malo* and little else. Away from family and friends, the young boys soon found themselves in these uniforms,

facing days that stretched twelve hours.

HBS linked the values of Calvinist industriousness and a New England industrialism to a future Hawaiians a few years before could never have imagined.

By the General Meeting in June 1837, David reported that twelve boys were enrolled, six of whom had graduated to attend Lahainaluna. By the end of the second year, 31 boys had attended HBS.

David worked extremely hard to make the school a success. His son Henry offered a glimpse of his father's day: "My father always rose at four o'clock in the morning and spent an hour in bathing, shaving, and reading the Hebrew Bible by lamplight. At five o'clock, the schoolboys were assembled for morning prayers; then, as the tropical daylight dawned, their teacher led them afield, where he directed their labors, planting and weeding or harvesting the crop, until seven o'clock, when all returned for breakfast. From nine o'clock till noon they were united in the school room. The hours between twelve and two were devoted to bathing and dinner. Then followed another session in school till four o'clock. An evening hour of farm work served to whet the appetite for supper, after which indoor recreation and music filled up the evening, till nine

o'clock, when all lights were extinguished and everybody went to sleep."

David handled school discipline just as he dealt with his own children, only resorting to corporal punishment for severe offenses. He firmly believed in having pupils discipline themselves, both as individuals and as a group, and wrote his brother: "I think it the best way, generally, to get along with as little corporal punishment as may be. Were I to teach again, I would resort to it less frequently than hitherto I have done. It is the best way, generally, to place so much confidence in scholars as to make them ashamed to do wrong."

The Lyman family about 1852. David and Sarah are surrounded by (left to right) Francis, Emma, Rufus and Ellen. This is the earliest known photograph of the Lymans, who had been living in Hilo some two decades by this time.

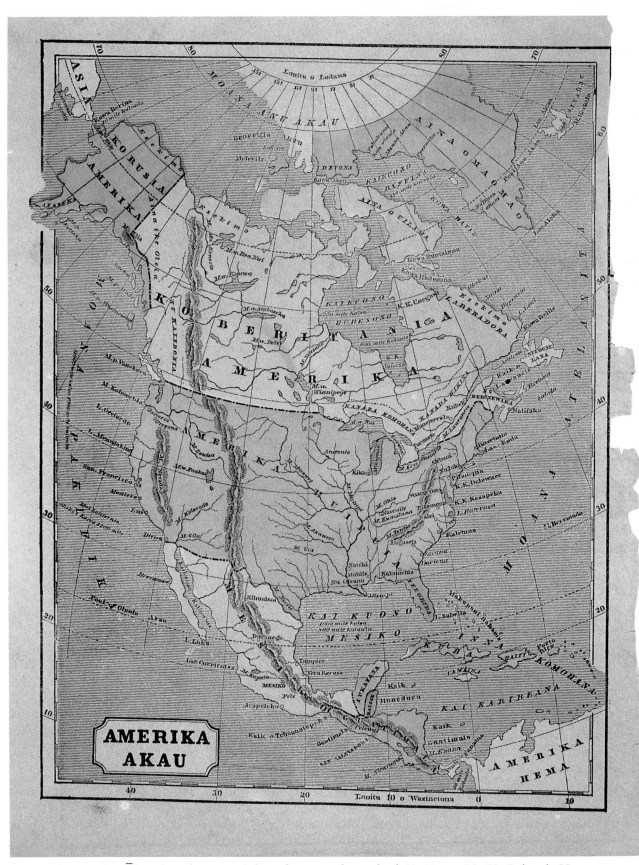

A map of 'Amerika 'Ākau (North America) from the geography textbook He Nīnau No Ka Palapala Honua.

David had the boys form a court to preside over rule infractions. He acted as advisor to the court, not as judge. He was a century ahead of his time here, and in his insistence that physical activity and vocational training went along with academic and religious training.

In 1838, Mrs. Fidelia Coan opened a boarding school for Hawaiian girls, in a small building erected near the Coan home, to provide a "sister school" to HBS. The girls were taught elementary academics, housekeeping and religion. It was hoped that they would marry HBS graduates and so create Christian homes. The girls' boarding school never had many pupils—and very few of those actually married HBS boys. Increases in Mrs. Coan's family and her own failing health forced its closing in 1846.

In 1837, the ABCFM sent Abner and Lucy Wilcox to assist in the schools around Hilo. Both were teachers and a welcome addition, but they were not physically strong. By his own admission, Abner wasn't much of a match for the

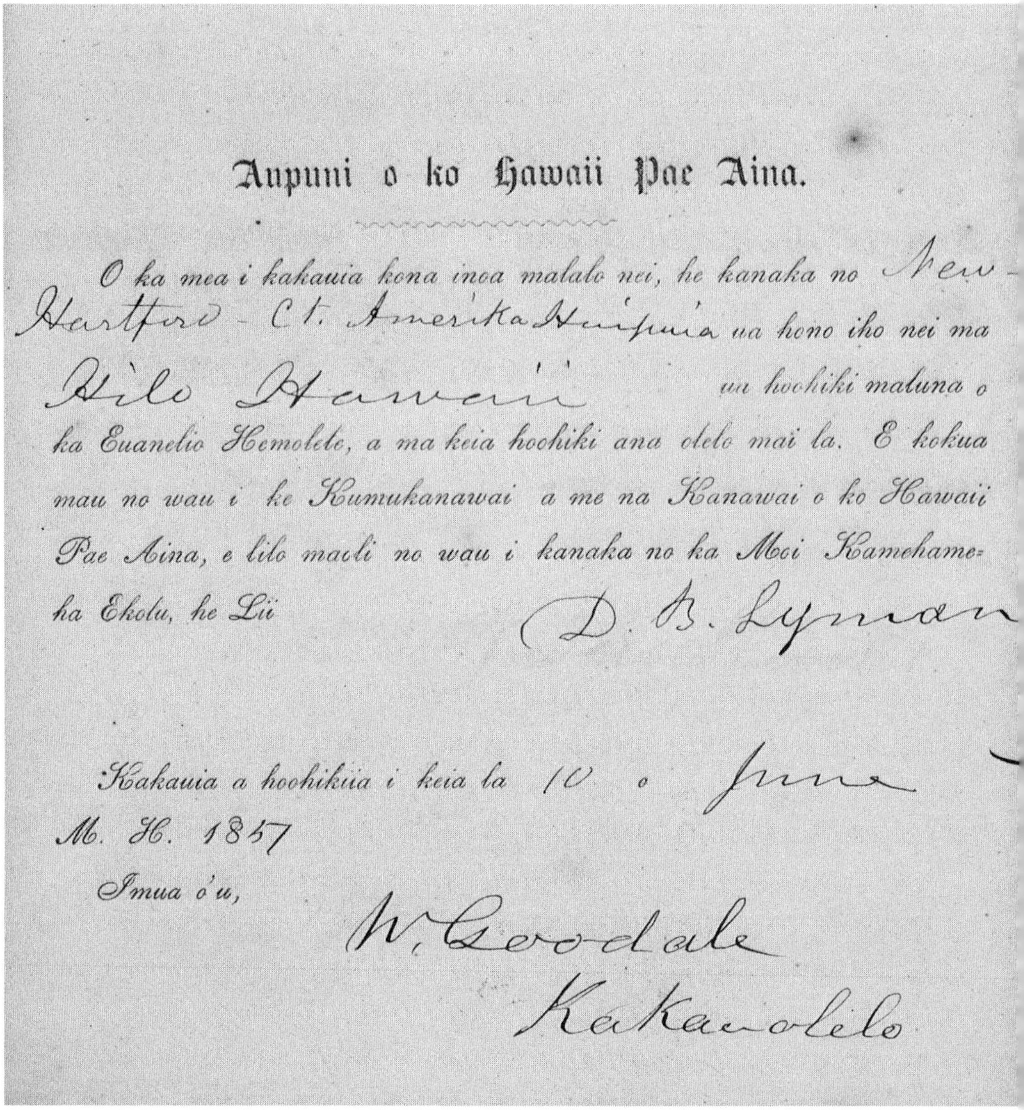

Aupuni o ko Hawaii Pae Aina.

O ka mea i kakauia kona inoa malalo nei, he kanaka no *New-Hartford - Ct. Amerika Huipuia* ua hoao iho nei ma *Hilo Hawaii* ua hoohiki maluna o ka Euanelio Hemolele, a ma keia hoohiki ana olelo mai la. E kokua mau no wau i ke Kumukanawai a me na Kanawai o ko Hawaii Pae Aina, e lilo maoli no wau i kanaka no ka Moi Kamehameha Ekolu, he Lii

D. B. Lyman

Kakauia a hoohikiia i keia la *10* o *June* M. H. *1857*

Imua o'u,

W. Goodale

Kakaolelo

tireless Coan, with whom he often went on trips to Puna and Hāmākua. Lucy was soon both pregnant and ill. They sailed to Honolulu for medical care and were away from Hilo for months at a time, impacting Abner's work in the schools. In 1844, the Wilcox family was transferred to O'ahu.

Enrollment at HBS increased during the Great Revival of 1838-39, and by November 1840, David reported to the ABCFM: "112 boys have been admitted to the school. They have to a considerable extent, been shielded from the temptations to which Hawaiian boys are usually exposed. Our efforts to train them to habits of industry have, for the time being at least, been successful beyond our most sanguine expectations.

"We have endeavored to impress upon them that God's authority is paramount to all others. We have at present 20 church members (in school). 4 entered Lahainaluna, 4 others have completed their course there. One joined a whaler, one (a part white boy) transferred to the O'ahu Charity School. Ten were enticed away by friends and their places filled. Three dropped out for

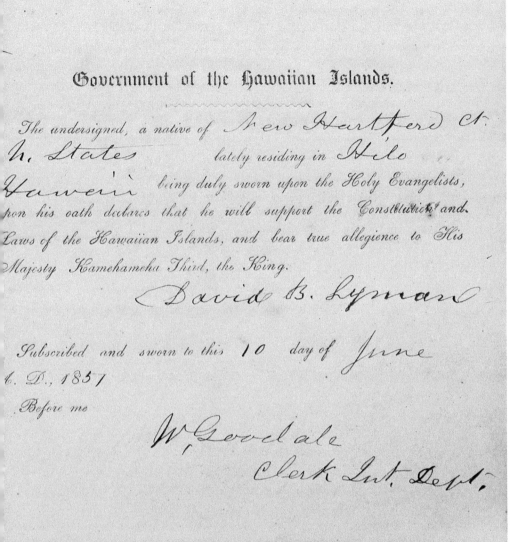

Government of the Hawaiian Islands.

The undersigned, a native of *New Hartford Ct.*
N. States lately residing in *Hilo*
Hawaii being duly sworn upon the Holy Evangelists,
pon his oath declares that he will support the Constitution and.
Laws of the Hawaiian Islands, and bear true allegience to His
Majesty Kamehameha Third, the King.

David B. Lyman

Subscribed and sworn to this *10* day of *June*
A. D., 1851
Before me

W. Goodale
Clerk Int. Dept.

health reasons, nine others because not promising, five expelled for misconduct."

J. J. Jarves, founder and editor of the early newspaper *The Polynesian*, described Hilo Boarding School: "They partly support themselves by their labors; all are neatly clothed and their whole appearance reflects great credit upon their instructors. They are lodged in a large thatched two-story building. The lower part is the school room; the upper is divided by mat partitions into numerous chambers for sleeping apartments. Besides this, there is another house of the same

Above: On June 10, 1851, David Lyman took the oath of allegiance to the Hawaiian monarchy and became a naturalized subject. This was at the urging of Dr. Gerrit Judd, missionary turned government official and with the approval of the ABCFM, which was then in the process of officially closing the Mission and releasing the missionaries.

size where they eat, after a civilized manner. They are allowed meats as often as they can be procured. For the sick there is a separate building where they can be retired from the noise of the school and have such attention as their wants require."

When a ship captain donated a bass viol to the School, Sarah learned to play it, then taught one of the boys, who played it in church. Sarah taught herself the flute, then taught the boys, who made flutes of bamboo. She also comforted the homesick, cared for the ailing, and taught boys to mend clothes. "I have for a long time as soon as evening prayers were over taken a cup of sulphur and molasses and the bottle of ointment which father sent

me, gone into the school room, dosed and anointed the boys, hoping to cure them of the itch." But Sarah's time was limited during these first few years, for six new Lymans arrived with some rapidity: Frederick (1837), David (1840), Rufus (1842), Ellen (1844), Francis (1846), and Emma (1849).

The ABCFM had allotted $500 for materials for both a permanent school building and a new principal's house. David purchased the entire cargo of the first ship to bring lumber to Hilo, and in 1839, the Lymans moved into the home where they spent the rest of their lives. This building had much native *koa*, as well as the lumber David had purchased.

Henry describes his boyhood home:

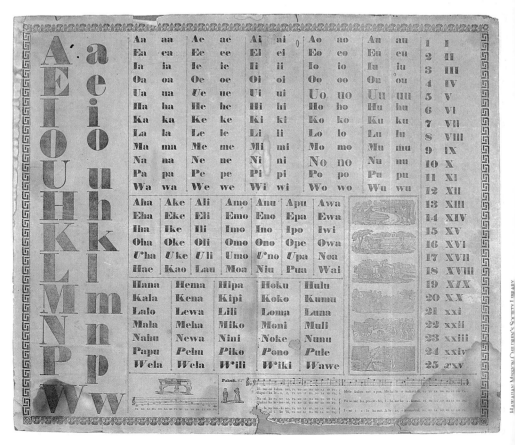

An early printed chart of the Hawaiian alphabet with its five vowels and seven consonants.

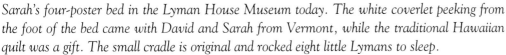

Sarah's four-poster bed in the Lyman House Museum today. The white coverlet peeking from the foot of the bed came with David and Sarah from Vermont, while the traditional Hawaiian quilt was a gift. The small cradle is original and rocked eight little Lymans to sleep.

"Our house, as we always styled the paternal residence, was a wooden building of one story placed on a stone foundation that surrounded a spacious cellar. There were four rooms on the first floor,...a dining room and common sitting room, and my mother's bedroom, on the front side, looking out upon the ocean. Behind our Mother's bedroom was a smaller bedroom for my little brother Fred and myself. Behind the dining room, opening out of a narrow passage that contained the stairs, was a small room for the storage of such articles as were used in barter with the natives for provisions; in fact it served as my father's office and reception room for such people as came on secular business. In the rear of all was a semi-detached kitchen, with an old fashioned open fireplace and an oven all constructed out of rough stones, bricks then being unknown in Hawai'i. Upstairs were two attic bedchambers with dormer windows, from which were visible the beautiful bay and the blue ocean that filled the whole northwestern horizon."

The roof—steep to shed Hilo's frequent rains—was originally thatched

57

Dedicated in 1859, Haili Church is the fifth (and last) Mission church in Hilo—the first four were thatched. This 1864 painting was done by visiting American artist Enoch Wood Perry.

and required almost constant repair. Later, the roof was quite literally raised, given a gentler pitch, and sheeted with "zinc" (galvanized iron). This provided four bedrooms to the upstairs for the growing family. A larger office for David was also added, with a separate entrance so people could meet him without disrupting the household's routine.

As the school increased in size and prestige, it faced some problems. In 1841, David reported: "A portion of land designed to be cultivated by the School has been taken the last year for the King's *po'alua* (land cultivated on Tuesdays for the King by his subjects as a labor tax). Should further encroachments of this

kind be made against which we have no security, operation of the school will be embarrassed and the expense increased." Kamehameha III had a legal right to the land, as Ka'ahumanu had only granted the missionaries permission to use it. The HBS trustees spent some anxious years until they finally obtained a charter in 1848 and then incorporated to obtain clear title to the School land.

In 1853, an arsonist torched the main HBS building. Teachers, pupils and townspeople fought the blaze, but it was a total loss. People throughout the Kingdom donated money, books, and materials. A temporary building was erected with lumber donated by Pitman's

General Store. Meanwhile, pupils were boarded in Hilo, the boys farmed as usual, and Sarah taught English at home.

Although by this time, the ABCFM had declared the Mission in Hawai'i a success and withdrawn direct support, David requested money to rebuild the School from the Prudential Committee, and was delighted to get $2,000. Noting the educational contributions of HBS, the Kingdom donated $4,000 to help get the School established again. David ordered a shipload of lumber from Oregon for the new school. Added to lumber donated locally, there was more than enough, so some was used to remodel and repair the Lyman home and the rest to build the fifth Haili Church.

The new building was uphill from the Lyman's home, and closer to the expanding farm, which had a variety of crops and a herd of dairy cows. In 1860, David described the structure: "A good substantial frame building with zinc roof, 2½ stories high, 52 by 30 feet with a projection of 20 by 30 feet in the rear,

containing school rooms and accommodations for the residence of a native assistant and 65 or more pupils, with a veranda in front 8 feet wide, floored above and below, also a stone basement containing a dining room and two store rooms."

It seemed likely that the Hawaiian government would take over HBS as it had Lahainaluna. This never happened, but HBS conformed to the government schools and gave classes in English, by then an official language of the Kingdom.

Both David and Sarah preferred to teach in Hawaiian—this helped the boys think of the School as their own rather than as one thrust upon them. The Lymans were beginning to see a need to prepare the boys of their School to be good Christian Hawaiians, instead of imitation foreigners alien to their own country. The more contact they had with the Hawaiian culture, the more good they saw in it. Their views had changed considerably from the time they first landed in Hawai'i.

Henry Lyman (silhouette at right) drew this picture of his home after the thatched roof had been replaced by galvanized tin and four second-floor bedrooms had been added in 1855.

60

The Second Generation

In the language of the times, Sarah bore David eight children. Certainly both had high hopes that their offspring would follow their missionary footsteps. None did, but all became responsible, caring citizens, and three helped educate future generations in Hawai'i.

Almost remarkably, considering the incidence of childhood mortality at the time, seven of the eight second-generation Lyman children lived to adulthood.

Growing up as offspring of New England missionaries, in the remote outpost of Hilo, theirs was not an ordinary childhood. The Lyman's son Henry, who became a Chicago physician, wrote a book called *Hawaiian Yesterdays*, describing the young Lymans' upbringing.

"The experiences of the Tahitian missionaries convinced the members of the Hawaiian mission that it was not safe to permit their children to grow up exposed to the coarse influences of the

Facing Page: Sarah is flanked by her two youngest children in this portrait taken around 1853. Sarah would have been about 48, while Francis (left) and Emma (right) about eight and five respectively.

wild inhabitants. The little ones were therefore kept as far as possible away from the natives. The only way of escaping these evils, during the early days of missionary work, was to send the children to their relatives in America. In several instances this had been done when the unfortunates were not more than seven or eight years old. But the trials of the parents, confiding their darlings to the care of rough sea-captains for a voyage of six months,—little girls even, having been thus sent without mother or female companion,—were too painful to be repeated. Torn shrieking from their mothers' arms, the wailing infants were hurried away, around Cape Horn, and sent to live among strangers, in order to preserve them from contaminating contact with Hawaiians. Their souls were saved, no doubt; they were safely handed over to their American kindred, and put in this way of getting a Christian education—but at what an expense of feeling!"

None of the Lymans were sent to the mainland until college. They were raised in Hilo and sent to O'ahu's Punahou School for further education. Punahou was founded by the Sandwich Islands Mission in 1841, on land donated by Kamehameha III, to educate the children of the Mission. All seven of the surviving Lyman children attended Punahou, just as

The Lyman Second Generation

David Brainerd Lyman
4-12-1834 to 7-28-1836
died aged 2 years
at Lahaina, Maui

Sarah did not get pregnant for more than a year after the Lymans arrived in the Islands. Their first-born son was named for a famous early missionary to New Jersey Indians.

On their way home from the 1836 General Meeting on Oʻahu, little David took ill and died at Lahaina. He was just over two years old. His father departed from his typical reserved remarks in his journal and letters to write detailed accounts of the little boy's passing, and Sarah still mentioned him years later. They even gave their fourth-born son the same name —a common practice at the time. Though the little boy's death had an enormous impact on the Lymans, they were comforted by the belief that he was among the angels and God's elect.

Henry Munson Lyman
11-26-1835 to 11-21-1904
Punahou School
Williams College
died aged 69 years
at Evanston, Illinois
Wf: Sarah Kittredge Clark
5 children:
Mary Isabella
Helen Cossitt
Julia Huntington
Margaret Hyde
Henry Munson Clark

Near the end of his Punahou career, Henry took time to come home and survey land for the Great Mahele. Some of his boundaries still hold on Hawaiʻi Island.

He then went off to New England and studied medicine at Williams, where his father had gone a quarter-century before. He graduated as class valedictorian and had a successful medical practice for years in Chicago.

His wife Sarah was daughter of an ABCFM missionary from Maui. Henry was an active layman in his local church and gave the first organ to the First Foreign Church in Hilo.

Frederick Swartz Lyman
7-25-1837 to 4-14-1918
Punahou School
died aged 81 years
at Hilo, Hawaiʻi
Wf: Isabella Chamberlain
6 children:
Ellen Goodale
Frederick Snowden
Francis Anderson
Levi Chamberlain
Ernest Evarts
Esther Rosalie

Named for a hero of the early days, who lost his life as a missionary, Fred became one of the great 19th century contributors to life in Hilo, carrying on the work of HBS as president of its board of trustees for 34 years. He was a civic servant, businessman and successful investor.

Fred married Bella Chamberlain, daughter of Levi, business agent of the Honolulu Mission. She grew up in one of the Mission Houses (today a museum) on King Street.

Two of Bella and Fred's children—Ellen and Levi—were involved deeply in HBS during their lives.

David Brainerd Lyman
3-27-1840 to 4-8-1914
Punahou School
died aged 74 years
at Chicago, Illinois
Wf: Mary Eliza Cossitt
4 children:
David Brainerd, Jr.
Franklin Cossitt
Mary Ellen
Paul Henry

Named for his deceased brother, who in turn was named after an early missionary hero, David helped Henry survey during the Great Mahele and helped earn enough to pay part of his college expenses.

Despite his parents' hopes that he become a minister, he chose law and practiced for years in Chicago, keeping in close touch with his brothers Henry and Francis. He was an active Episcopal lay worker and the father of four children.

Rufus Anderson Lyman
6-23-1842 to 7-4-1910
Punahou School
died aged 68 years
at Hilo, Hawai'i
Wf: Rebecca Hualani Ahung
Brickwood
15 children:
Lilian Louisa Hanakahi
Rufus Anderson Mahai'ula
Arthur Brickwood Keonelehua
Henry Joiner Kaleiokalani
Richard Jewell Kahekili
Eugene Hollis Kekahuna
Norman Kalanilehua
David Belden Kua'ana
Muriel C. Kaniu Hualani
Sarah Irene B. La'amaikahiki
Clarence Kumukoa
Rebekkah Agnes
Albert Kūali'i
Charles Bishop
Lewis Thornton

Named after the Foreign Secretary of the ABCFM who oversaw the Hawaiian Mission, Rufus spent his life on Hawai'i. Though the Lymans still hoped for a missionary son, he became a cane farmer, government official and businessman.

Ellen Elizabeth Lyman
9-27-1844 to 1-13-1868
Punahou School
died aged 23 years
at Chicago, Illinois
never married

Sarah and David's first daughter, Ellen attended O'ahu College (now called Punahou) after finishing her studies at home.

After graduation on O'ahu, she lived at home and taught English to some Hawaiian children in a nearby government school. Later she taught at HBS.

When she was 24, Ellen had saved enough money to visit her aunts and uncles in Illinois. There she contracted a high fever and soon died.

Francis Ogden Lyman
8-9-1846 to 12-16-1915
Punahou School
died aged 69 years
at Micco, Florida
Wf: Ruth Charlotte Dana
4 children:
Ruth Dana
Ruth Charlotte
Charlotte Dana
Richard Dana

Named for Miss Maria Ogden, a Third Company missionary who cared for him early in life. He assisted his brothers surveying and later went to the U. S. for further education.

Like his brother David, Francis became a Chicago attorney and an Episcopal lay leader. He married Ruth Charlotte Dana, daughter of author Richard H. Dana (*Two Years Before the Mast*). Late in his life, Francis retired to Florida.

Emma Washburn Lyman
9-16-1849 to July 28, 1934
Punahou School
died aged 85 years
at Līhu'e, Kaua'i
Hsb: Samuel Whitney Wilcox
6 children:
Ralph Lyman (Wilcox)
Lucy Etta (Wilcox)
Elsie Hart (Wilcox)
Charles Henry (Wilcox)
Gaylord Parke (Wilcox)
Mabel Isabel (Wilcox)

The youngest child, Emma taught at HBS for a time and then married Samuel Whitney Wilcox, son of Abner and Lucy Wilcox, who had been stationed at the Hilo Mission (1837-1844), before Emma was born.

Emma and her husband spent most of their married life on Kaua'i, where they were active in church, civic, and business affairs.

Emma was closely involved in the fight to save the Lyman House and make it a museum. She died at 85, both the longest-lived, and last surviving, of the second generation Lymans.

This dagguerreotype shows the Lyman's home in its 1839 form, with a steep thatched roof and two dormer windows. Much changed over the years, this is today's Lyman Museum House.

many do to this day, generations later.

As youngsters, the Lymans were pretty much confined to their home compound, cut off as much as possible from "contaminating native influences." They enjoyed their infrequent escapes. On clear mornings, Sarah might take them on before-breakfast walks to Hilo's beach to gather shells and enjoy sunrise. On Saturdays, they often walked to an ancient tuff-cone called Hāla'i Hill, where the children slid crude sleds down the grassy slope, while Sarah sewed or wrote letters in a shelter the missionaries built and called "The Bower."

As the children got older, there were jaunts to Rainbow Falls, to Coconut Island to picnic and swim, to an early Chinese sugar mill. Under the watchful eyes of missionary parents, they played freely with other missionary children, but not, of course, with Hawaiians.

Discipline for the little ones was sure and swift as Henry describes: "...on one occasion my mother gravely threatened to dip me under water in the tank in the bath-house if I did not get my lessons better. Despite my dread of this mode of baptism, I was soon delinquent again, and punishment followed without delay. I well remember the forlorn little figure that I presented, standing naked, dripping and sobbing, by my mother's side after immersion. Undoubtedly, she must have suffered more than the culprit from the infliction of this penalty, for she never repeated that form of punishment, no matter how great the offence.

"Dear mother! It was the tenderest affection that made her treat me so. She really thought that I should forever burn in hell, if not thoroughly quenched in water on earth. In those days everyone believed in the old proverb, 'Spare the rod and spoil the child'; consequently I and my younger brothers became well acquainted with the rod of correction before we were five years old. The flagellations we underwent were no trifling affairs, though we all grew to be discriminating judges of the difference between the strokes inflicted by the paternal hand and those that were given by our mother. In fact, we were some-times bold enough, when begging for a migration of sentence, to pray that she might be the executioner instead of heavy-handed papa. On one occasion, when six or seven years old, having been doomed to a flogging, I was ordered into the garden, myself to select an adequate mulberry stick for the rod. This was adding insult to injury; so with my little pocket-knife I made numerous subcortical incisions into the stalk of the twig, weakening the switch to such a degree that with the first blow it fell harmlessly in pieces across my bare legs. But though I had taken care to dance and howl most piteously in counterfeit pain, the fraud was immediately recognized, and I was straightaway made to smart most gen-uinely under the strokes of an infrangible rawhide riding-whip.

"These seasons of moral discipline were never undertaken in the heat of passion. We were always accused and tried with perfect deliberation, and if guilty, were sentenced to receive condign [worthy] punishment, usually the next day. This delay added greatly to the dread of execution, for the thought of a flogging in future does not swell the joy of the passing moment. Occasionally the sentence was forgotten by the busy parent, or a day of unusually good behavior might sometimes lead to a pardon and remission of the sentence; so that we always had those hopes to sustain us through a period of anticipation. But

Ellen was eight when she was "constituted a Life Member in the Hawaiian Missionary Society." Mission business agent Sam'l N. Castle later co-founded Castle & Cooke.

65

generally the domestic authorities were as inflexible as the Fates, and we received in full measure what had been decreed for our good."

Discipline aside, future generations will no doubt puzzle at the way we raise our young, just as many of the missionary ways seem incongruous to us. Boys studied Latin at the age of eight and Greek or Hebrew two or three years later, in the hope that they might become missionaries. The program for a little child's birthday party often included a temperance meeting. They do seem in step with today's fundamentalists, for children were forbidden to read works of fiction now considered classics and only permitted to read stories with a strong religious bent, such as *Pilgrim's Progress*.

Rufus Lyman

Evidently, the later Lyman children faced fewer restrictions, for by then a number of non-missionary American and British settlers were members of the Mission Church. The changing customs of these people led the Lymans—probably unconsciously—to adjust to the times.

All of David and Sarah's surviving children—both those who migrated to the Chicago area and the four who remained in the Islands—added to the family's already substantial record of community service. Of those four, Ellen was a teacher in Hilo and died as a young woman on a visit to Illinois, Emma spent most of her life on Kaua'i, while Fred and Rufus remained on Hawai'i.

Unlike Henry, Francis and David, who were further educated (and then remained) in the United States, Fred and Rufus returned to Hawai'i Island after finishing Punahou. Both contributed greatly to their community. Both also came to know and appreciate Hawaiians.

Rufus, in fact, not only appreciated

Becky Lyman

Hawaiians, he married one—Rebecca Hualani Ahung Brickwood. On her mother's side, she was a direct descendant of the great chief Kūali'i, a ruler of O'ahu and, according to legend, of the other islands as well. Kūali'i is said to have passed away in 1730 at the advanced age of 175. Becky's natural father was a merchant known simply as Ahung, one of the very first Chinese in the Islands. After Ahung died, her mother wed an Englishman named A.P. Brickwood, who adopted two-year-old Rebecca. She and her mother were both well-known in the Honolulu royal court, and Becky was a close friend of Lili'uokalani.

Rufus was both a government official and a businessman. His political rise was meteoric at first, and he was Hawai'i Island's Assistant Governor under both Kamehameha V and Lunalilo. David Kalākaua was less kindly disposed toward missionaries and their descendants, and he did not reappoint Rufus.

Rufus and Becky's Hilo home was often the scene of elaborate dinners for visiting royalty and other high officials. Rufus felt that his position required such hospitality, and both he and Becky loved to entertain. The parsimonious Sarah was predictably appalled at the expense and lavishness of these parties.

Becky Lyman was gracious and well educated. She was active in the Haili Church, as well as congregations in Hāmākua and Puna. She was also a loving wife and mother to her fifteen children, twelve of whom reached adulthood.

Above: This watercolor of the Lyman House about 1870 was painted by a Hawaiian HBS teacher named O. Hawii. By this time, the house, originally built in 1839, was in its present form—the thatched roof replaced and raised to add four bedrooms upstairs.

When Lili'uokalani was badly injured in a carriage accident on O'ahu in 1881, Rufus built a wide path—later known as the Queen's Walk—from the road to their lānai. Two original stones still lie on the Hilo Union School grounds.

Rufus was not a particularly successful investor. A railroad into Puna, in which he put some money, never paid high returns. His indigo plants came into production just as aniline dyes were beginning to replace natural ones. He abandoned an experiment in growing rubber trees, and a coffee venture ran into trouble when the price dropped sharply.

Fred, the other Lyman son to stay on Hawai'i, tried his luck for a short time in the California gold fields as a young man. Soon disenchanted with the risk, he came home and started Clover Ranch on land he owned in Ka'ū. In 1861, he married Isabella Chamberlain, the daughter of his parents' friends at the Honolulu Mission, Levi and Maria Chamberlain.

Newlyweds Fred and Bella had a two-day trail ride from Hilo to Clover Ranch. Their possessions lashed on a train of pack animals, they endured rough trails and scorching heat. Once at Ka'ū, they stayed in a thatched house until their frame one was ready. The glass windows and wide verandah of their home commanded views of ships at sea, flocks of sheep and goats and herds of cattle, and in back, a misty, steep-walled valley. Their furniture came by sea, and then by ox cart. Bella's remarkable new iron cook stove drew neighbors from miles around.

While rugged, Ka'ū's frontier life was certainly easier than that faced by the pioneers of the time in North America. Hawai'i's climate was very mild, and no fierce Indians or predatory animals lurked nearby. Clover Ranch became a tourist stop between Hilo and the spectacular eruptions at Kīlauea Crater. Bella fed and housed visitors from the humblest to the highest—including Mark Twain—all of whom enjoyed the Lymans' hospitality, provided some cash flow, and lessened the solitude of life in Ka'ū.

Fred and his neighbors helped each other during cattle round-ups and sheep shearings. With a reputation for good judgment and experience as a surveyor, Fred was often called upon to decide boundary disputes. Soon appointed a land appraiser, then tax assessor, he was offered

Rev. David Belden Lyman

a Circuit Court judgeship. In those days, a judge below the Supreme Court in the Hawaiian Kingdom was not required to have a law degree.

Bella was closely tied to their house and garden, especially after babies began to arrive. The loneliness in Ka'ū posed a problem, as Bella was naturally outgoing and had always been surrounded by relatives and friends. As the children grew, Fred romped with them (as his father had never done), and they often accompanied him on work rounds. He was known around Ka'ū as a very hard-working, conscientious man of integrity.

Perhaps because he had taken part in the Gold Rush, Fred approached business conservatively, eschewing quick profits. And Bella, the daughter of the Mission accountant, was very frugal, making over clothes until they almost disintegrated.

Ever fearful of debt, Bella strenuously objected when Fred suggested they borrow money to install a cistern to store rain water gathered from the roof. Until they had saved enough to buy it outright, she painstakingly conserved water during an extended drought.

The Lymans looked forward to "ship days" when letters and packages arrived, as well as new merchandise for the little general store in Wai'ōhinu. The mail also brought income from the sale of hides, tallow, wool and dried meat. The irregular arrival of these ships kept Fred and Bella in touch with the outside world.

Bella adapted to life at Clover Ranch, and the couple had four children there—Ellen (1861), twins Fred and Francis (1863) and Levi (1866). They especially began to appreciate native Hawaiians—

from whom both their own parents had so carefully tried to shelter them.

The pace in Ka'ū was sleepy, but nature there could be frightening. During a drought in 1865, fire leaped from a land-clearing operation some miles to windward. Fed by a strong breeze, it destroyed crops and thatched homes before it was extinguished near the ranch. Another time, volcanic smoke appeared high on Mauna Loa behind them. Lava flowed for a time, then disappeared. As smoking cracks opened further down the mountain, lava reemerged near Kahuku some miles southwest of the ranch.

As a city girl raised on the more geologically stable island of O'ahu, Bella

Sarah Joiner Lyman

A reunion in Chicago! This group portrait of second-generation Lymans was taken about 1890 when Fred and Bella visited the United States. Seated, from left: Mrs. Henry, Dr. Henry, David, Mrs. David. Standing, from left: Mrs. Francis, Francis, Bella and Fred.

had difficulty adjusting to such threats. In 1865 an earthquake did major damage, a preview of what would follow. In late March 1868, the ground began to shake. Houses and lava rock walls shattered from the tremors, some so strong people could not stand up without support, and had to lie on the ground. Cliffs slumped into the sea. The Great Earthquake was actually more than a week of quakes preceding a monstrous cataclysm on April 2.

When the big one hit, Fred and Bella's house lurched off its foundations, and a lava flow broke out near Hīlea to the north. Volcanic steam propelled a great mudflow which poured down the valley's slope and killed 31 people, and a tsunami swept the Ka'ū-Puna coastline, inundating entire villages.

Many Ka'ū residents, including Fred

and Bella, gathered on Nāhala's Hill nearby, and spent a prayerful night in fitful sleep. The next morning, they loaded a few essentials on pack animals and set off for Hilo. In Kīlauea, they spent the night with a kindly Hawaiian who gave shelter, water and food to all refugees who appeared at his door. A rider reached Hilo ahead of them and told of their imminent arrival. Rufus sent fresh horses, and Becky and Sarah hastily prepared food for the travelers, who arrived home to a warm welcome.

Fred and Bella decided not to return to Ka'ū. After arranging for his Hawaiian foreman to look after the stock, he kept tabs on the ranch when he visited the area during his official duties. Fred bought land in Hilo and built a home there. Two of their four children, the eldest Ellen and baby Levi, struggled at first with serious illnesses in the wet climate.

Rufus, at that time the Island's Assistant Governor, offered Fred a job, but Fred refused, partly because Bella counseled, "As to these offices under government, it is just as it turns, sometimes up and sometimes down." Her comment was prophetic, given the vagaries of Rufus' own career.

Bella was delighted to move into their own house. They stayed first at the Mission House, and she wrote her family that she "would be in perfect misery" if she had to go on living with Father and Mother Lyman, whom she described as critical, narrow-minded, and strict.

In Hilo, Fred demonstrated great energy as a businessman and community servant. He opened a leather shop, and helped by a Spanish craftsman, produced work of such quality that a saddle and bridle won first prize at the Centennial Exposition in Philadelphia in 1876. He worked hard for the First Foreign Church (now First United Protestant Church) and eventually became superintendent of Homelani (Heavenly Home) Cemetery.

He and Bella had two more children in Hilo, Ernest (1872) and Esther (1876), to bring their offspring to a total of six.

Fred soon became a Circuit Court judge and a director of both the First Bank of Hilo and First Trust Company of Hilo, later founding a Fireman's Fund insurance agency, Lyman and Watsun. He also joined the Board of Trade, and the Volcano Research Association. Perhaps most importantly, in 1873 Fred became a trustee of Hilo Boarding School.

The next year David Kalākaua was

elected to the throne. Much has been written of his 17-year reign, usually focusing on his personal life, for Kalākaua was a sporting man who enjoyed a friendly wager and a tipple or two. He truly earned his nickname, "The Merry Monarch." Fiscally, Kalākaua was not particularly responsible and overextended both his own and the Kingdom's finances. He tried to restore his people's traditional culture, which had been bludgeoned by Western influences, including those of whalers, traders and missionaries.

But Kalākaua was not a backwards-looking man by any means, for he was both an inventor and an innovator, who loved technology. He installed an early telephone system between 'Iolani Palace and his Boathouse, and he later wired the Palace with the first electric lights in the Islands. Fred Lyman was an innovator himself, and he approved of Kalākaua's encouraging corporations to make new technology available to the public.

In 1878, Fred returned from a U.S. tour with plans to install and operate a telephone system on the Island. He soon founded Hilo Telephone Company. In 1894, he had HBS install a small dynamo to power tools and fifteen lightbulbs. When Hilo Electric Light was formed later that year, the School furnished water for the generator in trade for stock. Later, Fred became president of HELCO.

He also saw potential for agriculture and leisure along the Hilo coast, and he promoted real estate and the farming of coffee, *pia* and cocoa. Some of the small farms foundered, but the sale of vacation beach lots called *Hale Kainehe* (House of the Rustling Sea) was quite successful.

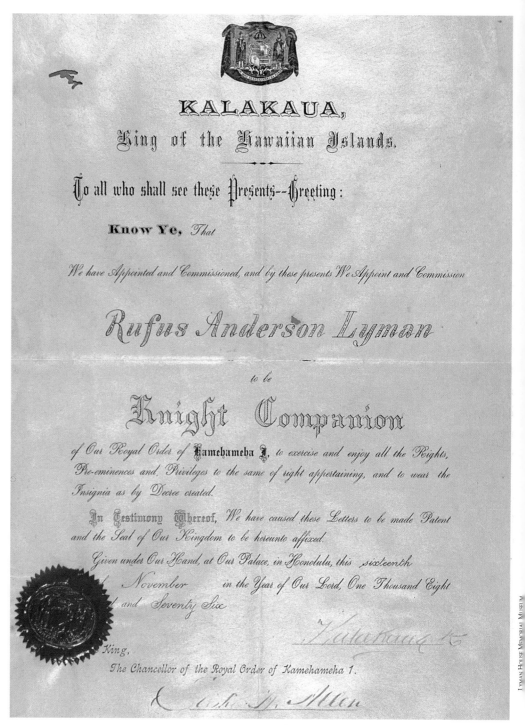

On November 16, 1876, Kalākaua's fortieth birthday, the king selected Rufus as a member of the Royal Order of Kamehameha I for his many years of service to the Hawaiian Monarchy.

In what may, in hindsight, be one of his most important influences on Hawai'i Island, Fred persuaded his friend Capt. William Matson to establish freight and passenger service between California and Hawai'i. This had an enormous impact on trade and on the Island's sugar industry.

Fred also donated land for Japanese Christians to build their first church, and land for Hilo's first free kindergarten.

Through the dynamic economic swings of boom and bust, Fred worked hard to keep HBS on a steady course, and his counsel proved essential.

Father Lyman died in 1884 at 81 and Sarah followed a year later at 80. Fred and Rufus and their wives were now the Lymans of Hilo.

For business reasons, Fred began to spend more time on Oʻahu, where he joined the Honolulu Rifles, a quasi-government volunteer militia whose commander, one Volney Ashford, once suggested inviting Kalākaua to present a prize and then shooting him. That suggestion went for naught, but in 1887, the Rifles helped force the King to sign a new constitution, effectively stripping him of all but ceremonial powers. The monarchy, which had been absolute 68 years previous under Kamehameha I, had slowly but surely disintegrated, first to a constitutional monarchy and finally to a figurehead. In six more years it would disappear altogether.

Fred himself was loyal to the Crown, and from 1880-88, he acted as clerk for Princess Likelike and later Princess Keʻelikōlani, Governesses of the Island of Hawaiʻi. But he disliked what he saw as fiscal irresponsibility and improprieties in the reigns of Kalākaua and his sister and successor, Queen Liliʻuokalani. When she fought to impose a new constitution to return more power to her, a coalition, heavily laden with missionary sons, engineered her overthrow. Although Fred took no part in the revolution, he did serve in both the Provisional and Republic governments. He was chosen to help draw up the new constitution in

1894 and served as senator from east Hawaiʻi from 1895 to 1898. After annexation to the United States, he became a patriotic American, making speeches to schools on loyalty and civic responsibility.

In May 1901, Bella died at 62. Fred's youngest daughter, Esther, kept house for him and taught school and music lessons until she married William McCluskey, principal of Hilo Union School. After the couple moved to the U.S., Ellen, Fred's unmarried oldest daughter, moved in to care for him while she taught at HBS.

Rufus served for years as a judge, and in 1909, he wrote in his diary that he had been continuously in government for forty-seven years, under three kings, a queen, a Provisional Government, a Republic, and finally a U.S. Territory.

In 1876, Kalākaua awarded him the Kingdom's highest honor, the Order of Kamehameha l. He spent his later years growing sugar cane and taking an interest in the young people of Puna and Hilo. In February 1906, his beloved wife, Becky, died, and Rufus followed her on July 4, 1910, aged 68. He had worked long and hard for Hawaiʻi Island.

Fred's son Levi was now principal of HBS, and Levi's wife was a teacher there, so Fred and Rufus were able to see the family carrying on the work their parents had begun over eighty years before.

The continuity of the Lyman gift to others was intact, and at his death on April 14, 1918, at 81, it was clear that Fred Lyman—jurist, innovator, businessman, and public servant—had made the life of his community much the better for his presence.

Sarah's Earthquake Book

EARTHQUAKES

Sarah Lyman was astonished by the earthquakes she felt in Hilo, and as a faithful observer of natural phenomena, she began to record them in detail. She had no idea how valuable her journal would one day prove, although even then her handwritten *Earthquake Book*—as it became known—has notations such as: "Copies to here for Dr. Winslow" and "Copied to here for French Consul."

While the French Consul may have been interested in Sarah's observations, today's geologists find them invaluable, because they were made during a period of great seismic activity and because they were so exhaustingly thorough. Sarah had no seismometers automatically recording tremors, of course, nor any Richter Scale of intensities as a guide, so she devised her own system.

Neither David nor Sarah often mentioned earthquakes in their letters home to New England—probably so as not to frighten the recipients—but Sarah laced her *Earthquake Book* with personal notes: "...It was a memorable night. We felt the shock not far from 12 (midnight) ...We arose and looked about the house and saw its effects on the plastering, milk, etc., and retired. About 1AM there was a jar and we sprang up expecting a heavy shock to follow but were disappointed; but our feelings had become too much excited to allow of our sleeping. We therefore dressed and sat up the [rest] of the night; and never shall I forget how

intensely I watched for the morning...Our plastering and chimney cracked and some stone walls thrown down.

On March 28, 1868, she noted five light quakes. The next day there were seven. The tempo was increasing. On April 1: "There were six shocks between the hours of eleven last night and six this morning. Have felt two during the day and a jar this evening."

Then BOOM, April 2, 1868: "Twelve shocks during the night, most of them easy. One, however, rocked the bed considerably. At four o'clock this afternoon there was such an awful rocking and heaving of the earth as we have never felt before. I noticed there were a series of shocks following each other in quick succession, the third of which drove us from the house. After a cessation of only one or two minutes, the fourth came, in which violent undulations, rotary and almost all other motions were combined or followed each other in quick succession...the surface of the earth seemed to move like the surface of the ocean and the large trees to sway hither and thither like ships' masts in a storm.

"The few stone buildings in the place were ruined. The chimneys of cook and dwelling houses were thrown down. Clocks, mirrors, and crockery, not firmly secured, were generally thrown down and broken. Cellar walls and underpinning were much damaged. Stone walls were generally prostrated, even the foundation stones being generally removed from their original position and it was not easy to

Earthquakes

"The earth rolls around and we take hold lest we fall."

A Hawaiian servant, telling Sarah why his handprints were on the door casing after a quake.

tell in which direction from the wall the larger portion of the stones had fallen. The best chimney stacks of the Hilo Sugar Mills were thrown down while some of the old cracked chimneys supposed almost ready to fall were little affected...the wonder was that any building was left standing."

TSUNAMI!

Sarah also recorded tsunamis and volcanos. A huge tsunami hit Hilo in 1837—during the Great Revival—when hundreds, perhaps a thousand, thronged into Hilo and were camped along the bay.

Sarah notes: "As we were about to kneel for prayers in the evening we heard a great outcry among the natives on the beach, concluded that there was trouble among the sailors of an English ship now in port. As soon as the prayer was over Mr. L. went to ascertain the cause of such confusion when to our great surprise we found that the water in the bay had risen ...beyond its usual bounds. A number of houses had been in an instant swept away and the inmates carried no one knew where. In a little time however they began to swim out to the water. Some had been carried a considerable distance...but owing to their skill in swimming had escaped a watery grave. The father came out of the water not knowing but that the other members of the family were all drowned and so with the mother and children. Some...were carried in one direction and some in another...

"In a canoe house was a large company of people from abroad to attend our meeting. The house was swept away and the people escaped with the skin of their teeth...Most people came out of the water as naked and destitute as they came into the world, without a bit of kapa to cover them or a place to lay their heads...The prevailing impression seems

Tsunami

"...a display of the mighty power of Him who holds the sea in the hollow of his hand."

SJL May 1841

75

to be among the people that it is a judgement from God, on account of their disregarding his word."

VOLCANOS

Volcanic eruptions are fascinating, and Kīlauea's fame as an active volcano which could be visited safely was widespread by the time the Lymans got to Hilo. Sarah frequently mentions visitors to Kīlauea who stayed with them in Hilo.

Sarah and David first visited Kīlauea in August 1833 with Samuel Ruggles, Dr. Dwight Baldwin and a company of Hawaiians. The men walked, while Sarah was carried most of the way in a *mānele* (hammock) suspended on a pole lugged by two men. She notes: "Eight men are engaged to carry me." They arrived at the crater's edge on the afternoon of the second day. Sarah continues: "At evening we repaired to the edge of the crater where we had a most splendid view of the fires. The crater is about seven miles in circumference at the top. It has sunk several hundred feet..leaving a black ledge several rods in width the whole circuit of the crater, so that people can descend and go around with comparative safety. At the bottom there are two lakes, one mile apart perhaps,...and this evening the fires were exceedingly brilliant. There appeared to be a current as in the ocean. The boiling lava flowed from one side to the other, the waves sometimes dashing to great height...There are large crevices in the ground in every direction, from whence issue smoke. The heat from them is sufficient to boil water, or cook food: About one half mile from the edge of the

Volcanos

"...saw the liquid fire flowing over a precipice, 30 ft. high, into a basin of water which might float a schooner."

SJL, Feb 1856

crater is a large sulphur bank".

Almost twenty years later, in a letter to Fred at Punahou, Sarah described the view of an eruption from their home: "March 2, 1852...This morning at a little past 4 o'clock finding your father awake I asked him how the volcano was, he arose, looked out, and returned saying, 'It is grand.' We called Henry and went to the roof of the cook room and lo it was...more luminous than usual, the crater considerably enlarged and tremendously active, a new channel was formed a little higher up the mountain in which a stream of lava was flowing a long distance toward Mauna Kea...the children are getting quite a crop of Pele's hair (fine spun lava) and we occasionally find cinders."

The Mauna Loa eruption of 1880-81 headed for Hilo. Sarah, then 74, took a keen interest in this eruption::

May 4, 1880 "Our far famed Mauna Loa is about 40 miles from here with nothing to obstruct our view...It looks as though the whole summit...is on fire."

July 27, 1881: "It looks now as tho' if...it gets below the cemetery, it will spread over the lower part of town, probably to the Wailuku River, so what will be left?

"Aug. 3, 1881. It seems now pretty evident to all that the lava will ere long reach the sea....A number of families have moved...Mrs. Wetmore has got nearly all her curios packed...Oh! It seems dreadful to think that we may yet see lava flowing down our streets like rivers of water and passing on to fill our beautiful harbor...

"Last night Luka, the old governess of Hawai'i, [Princess Ruth Ke'eliko̅lani] camped with a large number of people on the third hill and rumor was rife yesterday in regard to the incantations...to stop the flow. If she does not succeed, it will be because the "lands of Waiākea have been sold to haoles."

Ironically, the flow did stop, and Princess Ruth, who had never embraced Christianity, had employed the old chants of the Hawaiians' traditional religion to halt Pele. Sarah was not impressed:

"Aug. 16, 1881. Wonderful isn't it that the lava flow should have stopped so suddenly and died out so soon? Just as people were beginning in earnest to protect themselves, it cooled off...very soon all...fire and smoke disappeared...I think very many have been singing the doxology in their hearts ever since, whilst some few of the superstitious ones attribute the cessation of the flow to the influence of their chiefs."

In a letter from Sarah dated January 4, 1882: "lava flow ceased after coming within half a mile from us, and no light has been seen from it for four months, yet after a hard rain steam is seen rising from it almost the entire length of the flow..."

Bella took over the *Earthquake Book* (and noted: "Mother died December 7th 1885. Continued by B.C.L.") In both 1900 and 1904, the penmanship changed. The last entry was in 1916.

A disconsolate man identified as Captain Brown sits by the grave of his daughter, who was killed when her house collapsed into rubble during the cataclsym of April 2, 1868.

HBS...Ellen, Levi & Nettie

For almost exactly a century, Hilo Boarding School taught youngsters from the Islands, and later from around the world. There were many changes over the years, yet its one constant was the loving, committed attention of three generations of Lymans.

Hilo Boarding School opened in 1836, founded by then-33-year-old missionary David Lyman with the backing of the Sandwich Islands ABCFM Mission. As the school grew, its focus changed from training young Hawaiians as missionaries, to a vocational school, training them to compete in what was rapidly becoming a Westernized capitalistic economy.

Over the years, HBS went through a series of metamorphoses, in reaction both to outside conditions and financial considerations. At the very first, it was heavy on the four Rs (reading, 'riting, 'rithmetic...and religion), but within a few years, woodworking, blacksmithing,

and subsistence farming were added to the curriculum. Until the turn of the century, the student body was almost entirely Hawaiian boys. Later, it changed radically to serve Japanese and Korean immigrants who came to HBS specifically to learn a trade.

David and Sarah guided the school through natural and economic disasters and rapidly changing social conditions. Earthquakes and fires all took their toll.

During the 1860s, David's health declined, and in 1869 he first tendered his resignation as principal. Finding someone to replace him took five years, as it was hard to find anyone who even partially filled the requirements that David had outlined, "By principal, I mean the person who has to take charge of everything pertaining to the school 24 hours a day 365¼ days in a year, as teacher, treasurer, steward, etc, etc...there should be a man employed who may be expected to devote his life to the school"(David, of course, had done all this himself—for almost four decades.)

David served in an advisory capacity as both principal emeritus and treasurer of the board of trustees almost until his death in 1884. Sarah had retired from teaching at HBS at the same time as David, but she also remained actively involved until her death in 1885.

Facing page: Levi Lyman watches a student forging a horseshoe in the HBS blacksmith shop. In the days before autos became commonplace, blacksmiths shod horses for Hilo carriages and rural Island ranches.

Both Sarah and David had helped the School expand to serve more and more pupils, and over 800 boys had passed through the portals during their tenure. Many graduates became teachers, lawyers, government officials, and church workers. And, as they had so fervently hoped, a few even became missionaries, carrying the Gospel as far away as Micronesia.

The ABCFM had begun to withdraw support for the Mission in Hawai'i as early as 1848, considering its work over. David was still so deeply involved with HBS that they continued to pay his $800 annual salary—from an account called the Old Missionaries' Fund—all his life.

David and Sarah both lived to see their beloved school firmly established and see their children and grandchildren active in its work. Their son Fred was on the Board of Trustees for years, and his children, Ellen and Levi, and Levi's wife, Nettie, all worked at HBS.

Fred and Bella lived at Clover Ranch when she became pregnant with Ellen. Since Ka'ū had no doctors, Ellen was born on November 30, 1861 at David and Sarah's Mission home in Hilo. A year and a half later, Bella travelled to Honolulu to have the twins, Frederick

Mrs. W.S. Terry was the principal of Hilo Boarding School from 1890 to 1897. She made a collection of photos, including this one of model Spanish-American War warships floating in the HBS pond. Since the War took place between April and August 1898, this picture must have been snapped early in Levi Lyman's term as principal.

From the earliest days of the HBS, the boys cultivated crops both for their own table and as a profit-center for the School. The students are working in a taro patch, with enormous banana plants in the background. The machine is a rock crusher which was donated to HBS.

and Francis, at her parents' house. In 1866, Bella went to Dr. Charles Wetmore in Hilo for the birth of her fourth child. Levi Chamberlain Lyman was born December 16, at the Hilo Mission house.

During the Great Earthquake of 1868, two-year-old Levi narrowly escaped death from a falling house timber at Clover Ranch. When the family moved to Hilo, he was sickly for a time, but developed into an active youngster fond of music, the outdoors and his friends.

Levi showed early signs of a quick mind, great practicality and an easy way with people. With his older siblings away

at school, Levi was "big brother" to the little ones, Ernest and Esther. He learned to interest and guide young children, skills useful to him later in his teaching career. He attended Miss Cora's School, run by the granddaughter of Rev. H. R. Hitchcock, and took music lessons from the Coans' daughter Harriet.

At home, he helped care for the garden and the farm animals, and learned carpentry. On family outings to Coconut Island, he collected shells and rocks. As he grew older, he went horseback riding and boating with his father and hiking with his friends. Occasionally, he went

In January 1895, almost precisely two years after Queen Liliʻuokalani was overthrown, a counter-revolution to restore the monarchy occured on Oʻahu. Levi, who was then a 28-year-old teacher at Kamehameha, fought in the Citizens' Guard of Honolulu against the royalists, who were disorganized and quickly routed. This uprising led to the final abdication of the Queen. The rifle that Private Lyman carried during the action is pictured opposite.

with his Uncle Levi, who was stone deaf but a good companion and seemed to get along better with children than adults.

In his teens, Levi fished and hunted waterfowl for the family table. He also often guided his parents' houseguests around Hilo and up to the volcano. Levi had a life-long interest in volcanology. He was an early member of the Hawaiian Volcano Research Association, a group instrumental in founding the Hawaiʻi Volcano Observatory on the rim of Kīlauea crater.

Levi had a natural curiosity, and he was fascinated by machines, agriculture, woodworking, music—even helping his father and uncle "keep the books."

In 1883, seventeen-year old Levi became the sexton at the First Foreign Church of Hilo—perhaps because church fathers paid him just $100 a year, though he did as much work as his adult (and higher paid) predecessor. Still, Levi enjoyed the prestige that went with ringing the bell for church services and keeping the premises clean and repaired.

By late 1885, his sister Ellen had returned from the U.S. and started teaching at HBS. The family could now afford to send Levi to Punahou's Oʻahu College. Bella worried about Fred's health, as he worked so hard to earn enough for his children's education. His own lack of schooling made their education all the more a priority for him.

At nineteen, Levi was more mature and diligent than the average Punahou student. His academic record was good, and he also participated in group singing, theatricals and swimming in the new pool. Ever the "ladies' man," Levi carried a homemade buttonhook so girls could finish buttoning their high shoes after they scrambled aboard the carriage taking them to church on Sunday. He loved music and lent his tenor to the church choir and school glee club.

After graduating from Oʻahu College in 1888, he taught at Kamehameha School for Boys. He realized that—in part due to his father's efforts—the Age of Industry was arriving in the Kingdom. Always inquisitive, he wanted to learn more about mechanical and electrical devices, so he took a leave of absence in 1890 to attend Pratt Institute in Brooklyn New York. He returned to Kamehameha Schools in 1892 to help the boys prepare for employment in the newly-developing economy.

About this time, a young lady from La Porte, Indiana arrived to teach at the Maunaolu School for Girls on Maui. Her name was Nettie Hammond, and her cousin, Rev. William D. Westervelt, was pastor of Wailuku Union Church and suggested her for the job. She taught there for a time and then transferred to Kamehameha School for Girls. Although

Kamehameha's Boys and Girls Schools were separate institutions, Levi met Nettie at various faculty functions. They were well-suited to one another, with many common interests, ideals and activities. Both were outgoing. Although Nettie had been reared on a farm in Indiana while Levi had grown up some four thousand miles away in tropical Hilo, their upbringings had been strikingly similar, and they both loved teaching young people. Their friendship soon fanned into romance, and they married in Honolulu on July 6, 1897, soon after Levi was appointed principal of HBS.

By that time Levi's older sister Ellen was 35 and had been teaching at HBS for twelve years. Ellen Goodale Lyman was tall, graceful, motherly and quietly efficient. She was not nearly so dynamic as Nettie, preferring to work behind the scenes. She never married, though her mother's letters to her seem to point to an unhappy romance in early adulthood.

Despite their very different personalities, Ellen and Nettie became very close friends. They were careful never to intrude in each other's *kuleana* (area of interest or responsibility). Nettie and Ellen were both active in community organizations, though they made it a rule never to hold office in the same group at the same time. Their close friendship was based on mutual respect and cooperation, that was designed so that there would never be competition—either real or imagined—between them. The rules were very clear: If either one of them had a special recipe, the other never served it. And neither interfered with Levi and his policies at HBS.

Levi and Nettie's first child, Kathryn Isobel, was born at HBS on July 11, 1898, a few days after their first anniversary. That fall, Nettie began teaching at HBS alongside Levi and Ellen.

Like businesses, private schools go through cycles of growth and decline, struggling to adapt to changes in the communities they serve. When Levi became principal, he was familiar with the operations at HBS, but the school population had dwindled 36 pupils and four teachers. The Lyman team—Levi, Nettie and Ellen, with Fred Sr. heading the HBS trustees—set out to enlarge enrollment, expand programs, and raise needed money. By the end of his first year as principal, Levi was able to report: "The school has greatly benefitted by the

change made this year of providing a home for teachers on the grounds—details of boarding school life, by this means, have been systemized—with daily inspection...and cleaning of dormitories and classrooms, mending and overseeing the clothing of the small boys, the weekly prayer meeting, and weekly teachers' business meeting and reading circle." Clearly teaching demanded more than eight hours in those days.

Capital improvements helped both the curriculum and the teachers. "Under improvement this year we may mention a new five-horsepower electric motor, a new forge shop, two new anvils and forges, a new poi machine, furnishing teachers' quarters, also a stone and cement swimming tank...is now in the progress of construction...The work scholarship program adopted this year was readily accepted by the boys."

This innovative program provided a way for boys whose parents could not pay all or even part of the tuition. A boy could work for the School, with his labor credited toward tuition. He could earn extra money by working outside of school, delivering surplus milk from the School herd, or peddling fruits and vegetables not needed in the kitchen.

Levi saw the value of learning money management and commerce early. A greater share of money earned went toward tuition, and a small portion for personal use, with boys and teachers noting the transactions. Levi ran the School bank and managed its store, encouraging boys to deposit their money, withdraw it by check, plan purchases and keep records.

LYMAN HOUSE MEMORIAL MUSEUM

Six Hawaiian youths pose for a photo after their graduation from HBS.

During a Study Hall, Levi supervises a group of students. He is seated between portraits of his late grandfather and of the original ABCFM committee which sent missionaries to the Islands.

Nettie was a good administrator and businesswoman, with great attention to detail and efficiency. Her special interest was the School's wonderful woodshop, and she enthusiastically encouraged the fine craftsmanship which made the shop famous. Like most of the other vocational classes, the woodshop's products were for sale to the general public, and even today, over half a century later, HBS furniture is prized in Hawai'i. The shop grossed thousands of dollars during its thirty-some years' of existence, and helped support other HBS programs.

Nettie was admired by her students. Several later became teaching assistants and a few joined the faculty as teachers. One, Tadaichi Shintaku, took Nettie's place when she retired in 1922. Eleven years later, he bought out the shop and ran it as a private enterprise after HBS was reorganized.

Nettie's multiple talents forged a link between HBS and the community. Her printing press class prepared brochures, programs, announcements, classroom materials, reports and advertising pieces both for the School and for outside organizations. For years, no other shop in Hilo was equipped to do this work, and this business brought income to the School and gave the boys experience.

Nettie took in every detail and played no favorites, and she kept in touch with many of the HBS students long after they had graduated.

Nettie also served as Levi's secretary and as the HBS librarian. She took care of the files, classified and repaired books—even reprinting torn pages—and prepared classroom materials. She also occasionally served as publicity agent and official fund raiser and wrote articles for local and mainland newspapers and magazines to help raise money. Her meticulous records leave a clear picture of Hilo Boarding School.

On November 19, 1903, Nettie bore her second child, Orlando Hammond Lyman. This fourth-Hawai'i-generation Lyman would carry on the long family tradition of serving the Hilo community.

Levi was busy with the School's administration, its machine shop and agricultural courses, and the constant struggle of a non-profit institution to stay afloat. Enrollment rose, and new teachers were added. In 1901 the School outgrew its main building (built in 1856), but it took four years to move the old structure and erect a larger one. By 1905 the trustees had enough money to put up the main framework of the new building. Volunteers, as well as students who were learning carpentry and plumbing, added the finishing touches. The boys poured a

The woodworking shop—run so well for so long by Nettie Lyman—was the School's most important profit center for years. Here boys are sawing and planing wood, while the youth on the right affixes a top to an unusual trestle table. This photo, like many of the others in this chapter, appears to be posed—to be used as illustrations for some of Nettie's articles, a catalog or a fund-raising brochure.

Tools at the ready, HBS boys head out to cultivate, or perhaps harvest, their crops. There is a wide variety of ages, ethnic backgrounds and dress—from the paniolo-*look of the boy with his hand on the wheel, to the straw "boaters" worn by the two young gentlemen at right.*

cement floor for the basement, and the plumbing class dug a cesspool and ran water pipes to the kitchen. Others graded and resurfaced the roadway. Building codes were not yet in force, so this work by students was legal. The building was dedicated in late 1905, though the new dorm lacked beds, and many classrooms needed painting and furniture. Students moved in anyway and roughed it.

The sizeable debt on the building led Levi, Nettie and the faculty to embark on new fund-raising ventures. Nettie wrote more letters and articles, and had the printing class print leaflets about HBS. A School Fair netted a thousand dollars, and plays and musicals brought in more.

Within two years, the debt was paid off, but donations kept coming in, and the endowment grew. Levi observed the strictest economy to keep the operation "out of the red," and in 1907-08, Levi and Nettie took a year's leave of absence. Leaving HBS in Ellen's capable hands, they took both children and went to Hampton Institute in Virginia to teach.

Hampton Institute's late founder, Gen. Samuel C. Armstrong, patterned the Institute after HBS. He had grown up in the Islands, the son of Fifth Company missionaries, Rev. and Mrs. Richard Armstrong. In 1851, Rev. Armstrong was the monarchy's Minister of Public Instruction and brought 15-year-old

No. 144. Hilo Boarding School, HILO, HAWAII.

This hand-tinted original postcard shows the main HBS building, probably in the 1920s. Note the covered lānais and stairways, designed as shelter from Hilo's often present rain.

Samuel to Hilo to inspect HBS. In 1868, soon after the Civil War, Samuel became the first principal of Hampton, founded by the American Missionary Society to educate Indians and Negroes. An early Hampton grad, Booker T. Washington, went on to establish Tuskegee Institute in Alabama to train "the head, the hand, and the heart" of Negroes. The influence of Hilo Boarding School was widespread.

While at Hampton, Levi taught agriculture and surveying, while Nettie concentrated on academic subjects. The next summer, Levi took a refresher course in shop work and bought new farm and shop equipment to bring back to Hilo. He and Nettie also renewed their ties with relatives in the United States.

In Washington, D.C. Levi met with President Teddy Roosevelt and Hawai'i's representative to Congress, Prince Jonah Kalaniana'ole, to request some obsolete

Spanish-American War rifles for military drill by HBS boys. Levi had reorganized this drilling based on his experience with the Citizens' Guard of Honolulu. With new uniforms and drill routines, the boys were in demand for local parades.

Since its founding, the School had always stressed teaching native Hawaiian boys, some of whom were too old to be accepted into public schools. Levi gave preference to them when enrolling new students. Earlier, a few older Oriental students, primarily boys who wanted to learn English and prepare themselves for a particular trade, were also accepted as students. They did so well that others clamored for the same privilege.

Levi always felt that HBS's major goal was to build character—industry, pride in workmanship, honesty, the ability to work without supervision and as part of a team, citizenship, respect for others, and reverence for God. Religion was not stressed as it had been in David's time, but it remained central, and the old HBS customs endured: daily chapel services, a weekly prayer meeting, Sunday morning services, Sunday School, and a Sunday afternoon prayer meeting.

The daily school schedule was as rigorous as it had always been. Boys rose at 5:30AM, worked farm or household chores until breakfast at 7:30, then attended health inspection at 8 and chapel at 8:30. From 9:10 to 12:15 students studied in academic classes.

After lunch, from 1:30 to 3, agricultural and other practical classes kept them busy. Shop classes stretched until supper at 5, and study lasted from 6:45 until taps sounded bedtime at 9.

After graduation, HBS alumni took many paths. A few were recruited as teaching assistants, then joined the faculty full-time. Others continued in the trades they had learned at HBS. Some pursued further education and became professionals, while still others were businessmen or government employees.

Though few graduates farmed, Levi

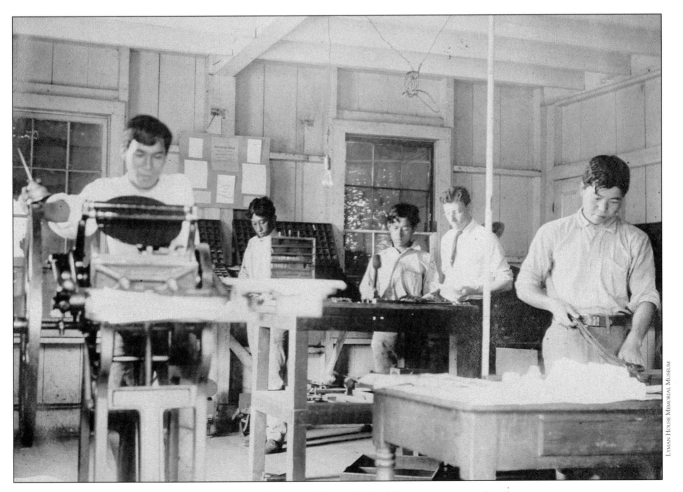

Nettie's other profitable vocational class was the print shop, which did items not just for the School but for sale to the community. Here, the boys learned to set type and run the presses. The teacher (in the tie in background) was Mr. J.O. Warner, who also served as chaplain.

built the dairy herd up and emphasized subsistence farming. A natural experimenter, he tried new forage plants and new varieties of sweet potatoes, taro, bananas, avocados and other crops.

Like his father, Levi firmly believed in the value of physical recreation. Saturday afternoons, holidays, and short vacations were devoted to games, hikes, picnics or swimming at Coconut Island. Longer hikes took the older boys up into the mountains on camping trips. Levi accompanied the boys, instructing them in camping skills and in the history, botany and geology of the Island. Kilauea Military Camp near the summit crater was a rallying place for camp events.

In 1916, professional contractors put up the framework of a gymnasium on campus. Carpentry students finished the building, and the first gym in Hilo became a favorite place for evening and

The HBS Crafts Room was where school projects were sold to the public. The tremendous variety of items is seen here—ukuleles, calabashes big and small, chairs, tables, clocks, desks, a rocking chair, even a cart. Each item was stamped with an HBS logo, and many were built out of the native koa from the upland forests.

rainy day activities. The extra-curricular program at HBS developed winning track, baseball and basketball teams, in part, perhaps, because many of the boys were older than their competition. Glee Club and drama filled out the program. Academically, the School library offered books, a phonograph and records, a magic lantern and a stereoscope.

Outwardly, the School was a great success, known throughout Hawaiʻi, the U.S. mainland and the Orient. Still, Levi and the trustees faced many difficulties.

Disputes and litigation with Hawaiʻi County over water rights to the HBS Ditch continued for years, as did problems over the right to use ditch water to generate power at Hilo Electric Light. (Levi was also a HELCO director, so this called for adroit handling.) Kamehameha III had granted the Hilo Mission and Boarding School half of the water of the Wailuku River for their use. Fortunately, this was in writing, so court judgement gave HBS 5,590,000 gallons per day.

The Territorial government also wanted some seven acres of HBS land along the Wailuku River for a new public high school. Some Legislators and the Governor questioned the School's legal right to any of its land on the grounds that no one held land in fee simple at the time the king had granted it.

Levi made several trips to Honolulu armed with the precious documents and land grants. There, he and the trustees met with the Governor and legislators and compromised. HBS gave up the seven acres in return for a small parcel of land near the School, plus fee simple title to the rest of the School lands.

LYMAN HOUSE MEMORIAL MUSEUM

By now both the faculty and student body had increased, and the endowment —$40,000 when Levi took office in 1897—had grown to $160,000, but the operating costs also continued to rise.

Other charities competed with HBS for funds, and public and private schools

A dapper Levi behind the wheel of the family phaeton during their trip across country. Note the extra spare tires on the back. Inset: The car after being converted into a tent.

competed with HBS academically as well, offering courses in agriculture, wood-working, machine shop and business. The Marianist Brothers founded a Catholic boys school, and a Catholic priest opened a boys' boarding home nearby. People no longer thought of HBS as the only place where young men could get a good education, nor did they feel an urgency to support it. Like many other non-profits, HBS was hampered by a lack of capital.

Newer members of the School's Board were alarmed at high per-student costs—especially in the vocational classes with just a few students. Some suggested reorganizing with a smaller budget, while others, including Levi, disagreed. With the popularity of the automobile, he saw a clear need to upgrade the curriculum. In 1917, Levi left George A. Young as acting principal, and took a sabbatical to Detroit to learn automobile mechanics.

The Lymans shipped their automobile to the mainland and booked space for themselves aboard the same freighter, a trip that took 13 days. Cross-country travel by automobile in those days was a major adventure. Once in San Francisco, Levi prepared the vehicle for the long drive and improvised a tent that attached to the side of the car. They packed folding cots for Nettie and 19-year old Kathryn, and modified the car's front seats so that they folded back to the rear seat forming a bed of sorts for Levi and 14-year old Orlando.

The journey was historic, for the Lymans were among the first families to drive—and camp—by auto from San Francisco going east, pioneers in reverse. Along narrow, rutted, often unpaved roads, they battled flat tires, breakdowns miles from anywhere, deep, cloying mud, and even snow in the Rockies. But free from the tensions he'd left behind in Hilo, Levi's health improved quickly. He loved camping, and Nettie and the children were great traveling partners.

When they reached Detroit, Levi enrolled in Michigan State Automobile School and studied repair and mechanics of the newer cars. Orlando learned how to rebuild tires, and attended public school. Kathryn took some courses as well, and Nettie visited cabinet makers, furniture dealers and antique shops hunting for different styles and patterns to bring back to her woodworking classes.

When the school year was over, the Lymans drove down to Washington D.C. and then around the Chesapeake Bay, touring the countryside. They bought a new car—which they shipped to Hilo rather than risk on the road—and took a train to San Francisco, then a steamer home to Hilo, arriving in time for the fall term at HBS.

That fall, a world-wide influenza epidemic hit HBS full force. The new gymnasium became a hospital, with unstricken teachers and older students serving as nurses. Students had left school to join the war effort, and enrollment was down. The agricultural department had just one mule (from three), and students had to cannibalize parts from several old cars to build a badly-needed truck.

When the war was over, enrollment boomed and by 1921, it had reached 140, though there were dormitory beds for just 100, and some older boys had to live off campus. Education suffered, and for 1922,

Boys learning both theory (note the blackboard) and hands-on automotive mechanics at HBS.

Hilo Boarding School Graduation Day, 1912. These four young men stand proudly wreathed in leis, clutching their diplomas and HBS pennants. On the right is Sam Lujan, who later joined the School faculty.

enrollment was capped at 100. By now, most of the boys were Orientals, primarily from Japan and Korea. They were bright and hard-working, and several later became teachers and department heads.

The Lymans retired after the 1921-22 school year, and Levi joined the Board of Trustees. The new principal of HBS, George Hargraves, was shocked by the School's constant struggle to make ends meet, the hybrid truck, the worn-out printing equipment. He was not of a frontier mindset and so was not used to recycling, improvising, and "making do." He was astonished that rather than buy inexpensive new dishes, old rusted ones were still used, some with pieces of paper over the holes to keep food in.

Hargraves was well-liked and hard-working. After two years he moved to Punahou, which was better off financially. His most important decision—to send students to public school for academics and focus HBS on vocational skills—substantially cut expenses.

The trustees could not find a new principal, and students welcomed Levi back as acting principal for a year while the search went on. Meanwhile, the local Japanese-American community showed its appreciation for all that HBS had done for its children. Led by Y. Okumoto, who headed the HBS shop, and students of the Morning Star Club, they started a drive for a new shop building. It took a while, because cash was needed for earthquake relief in Japan, but on May 27, 1924, Okumoto turned over $4,451.60 to the trustees, earmarked for a new shop. Levi was deeply touched and very grateful.

By 1925, Levi was no longer closely associated with the School. Most students were older boys who came to learn a trade. In 1927, a fire swept the old shop building, and the small Hilo Fire Dept. arrived too late to save it. HBS never completely recovered from the fire. Given the losses and the competition, the school sought survival in a new role—providing social services and recreational activities to the community. Levi oversaw the purchase of land for the School's Hilo Community Center in the densely-populated poorer section. HBS hoped to provide recreation and social services for young children and teenagers.

Still active in the community, Levi remained a director for Hilo Electric Light, Hilo Gas, First Trust Company, Hālaʻi Hill Land Company, and Hawaiian Insurance and Guaranty. He was also on the advisory board of the Hilo branch of Bank of Hawaii, an active Mason, a trustee of First Foreign Church. Like his father before him, he ran the Homelani Cemetery, where he added property, a crematorium, and a columbarium.

For years, Levi and Nettie had spent summers and vacations at their home in Volcano, *Haleʻohu* ("house of the mist which Pele wrapped about herself when she came up from the sea"). Fred, Levi, Nettie and Ellen built the home around 1901, and it served them for some forty years. Ellen loved *Haleʻohu*, especially the

garden, where she grew temperate-zone flowers which did not do well in tropical Hilo. Levi spent time at the Hawaiʻi Volcano Observatory with scientists, collecting data and taking notes for his frequent talks in Hilo.

The thirty miles of rocky, winding road from town to the isolated Volcano community seemed like hundreds. For years there were no stores, so food and supplies were shipped by train to the Glenwood station, then transported by stagecoach or private vehicle. Electricity was from generators. People cooked over a wood or kerosene stove and heated their homes with fireplaces or Franklin stoves. Candles and oil lamps gave light. The phone at Volcano House served in an emergency. Volcano was too chilly and damp from late fall to early spring so Levi and Nettie spent that part of the year at their Hilo home on Hālaulani Place.

After 1930, Nettie devoted herself to the Lyman House Memorial Museum. She arranged for several of her clubs to meet in the new Museum, both to build interest and to seek out artifacts. It was said that Levi and Nettie never threw anything away, which, while not precisely correct, does help account for all the documents and artifacts we still have from the early Lymans and HBS.

Meanwhile, Hilo Boarding School slowly disintegrated. Bits and pieces were closed down or sold off, including the woodshop. The School had served the Islands (and the Pacific) well, just a few years shy of a century. The Lyman family's community efforts shifted to the task of preserving the old Mission House and turning it into a museum.

The Lymans Establish a Museum

From Mission to Boarding School to Museum, the Lyman family's commitment to contributing to Hawai'i Island has been on-going for eight score years, and counting.

W hen the ABCFM phased out financial support of the Hawai'i Mission in 1863, they transferred land ownership to the station missionaries. David Lyman thus gained title to his home and other mission land. Kamehameha III presented him with some acreage in appreciation of his unpaid service to the Kingdom as examiner and virtual superintendent of the government and Mission schools within his district. And David himself later purchased more property.

After his death in 1884, the Hāla'i Hill Land Company was formed to administer the lands in David's estate. His heirs owned stock in the company, rather than the property itself, as many of them no longer lived in the Islands.

As HBS changed in the 1920s, the School itself no longer needed so much acreage, and increasing demand for new homes in Hilo led the Land Company to plan a subdivision there. The main road would logically be an extension of Haili Street—passing directly through David and Sarah's old Mission home. The Lyman heirs did not want the house demolished. David and Sarah's only surviving child, Emma (Lyman) Wilcox, was in her 80s and especially distressed, as were her three daughters, Lucy, Elsie and Mabel.

After Emma's husband died in 1929, these four set up the Samuel Wilcox Trust in his name and helped Levi and Nettie buy the old home, which had passed from the family years before. They felt making it a museum would be a fitting testimony to the family's contribution to the spiritual and educational life of Hawai'i.

The Wilcoxs wanted the street to skirt the property, so the home could stay on its original site, but the county insisted the street be straight. The old home was partially dismantled and moved nearby. It was shifted ninety degrees, and now faces the new Haili Street instead of the sea. The house was in surprisingly good condition considering its age (1839) and the tropical climate. During the move, the basement was eliminated, but otherwise the building was identical to when

Facing page: A portable writing desk is set up on a tabletop in the first floor front room of the Lyman Mission House Museum, just as it might have been when Sarah and David were penning long letters to loved ones far away. The inkwell contains a quill pen.

LYMAN HOUSE MEMORIAL MUSEUM

The Lyman Mission House in 1926, four years before it was re-purchased by the family, then dismantled and moved to the right of the Haili Street extension. The house here faces Hilo Bay, but it was turned ninety degrees during re-assembly and now faces the street.

David and Sarah lived there.

A board of trustees was formed for the budding museum, with Emma Wilcox as honorary president, and her daughters honorary vice-presidents. Emma herself was too ill to take an active role in museum affairs. By 1934, she and Lucy had both died, but Elsie and Mabel remained active in the Museum for years. A close family friend, A.S. LeBaron Gurney, manager of the Bishop Bank in Hilo, was elected president of the board.

The first six months of 1931 were a blur, preparing the old home for its new role as a museum, without losing its integrity and atmosphere. Items for display began to pour in, and Nettie and her committee cataloged, repaired and prepared them for exhibit. Anne Scruton was hired as the first curator, and she and her retired husband—known to all as Smiling George—moved into the little apartment adjoining the house in April. A capable, willing (and unpaid) Jack-of-all-trades, George was a great help in getting the Museum ready for its Grand Opening on June 20, 1931.

Meanwhile, Levi and Gurney were granted exemption from Territorial taxes and persuaded Hawai'i County to allow them free water. Finally, all was ready. Opening Day ceremonies were a great success, and 178 people signed the guest register. Hawai'i Island had a museum!

In 1932, a Centennial Celebration marked the Lymans arrival in Hilo in 1832. Sarah's old melodeon played her favorite tunes, the HBS chorus sang, and a commemorative bronze plaque was unveiled in front of the house. A rose and maile lei festooning the plaque was cut by some Lyman great-grandchildren. (The lei's small pink "volcano roses" were descended from those a sea captain presented to Sarah and which bloomed profusely in the coolness up at Volcano.)

Priceless artifacts were added to the Museum—early feather leis, Princess Nāhiʻenaʻena's tapa, and the "love flag quilt" sewn by Queen Liliʻuokalani's loyal friends, who had voluntarily shared her imprisonment in ʻIolani Palace. Rare Bibles and other memorabilia of the early missionaries were given by members of the Hitchcock, Bond, Coan, Wetmore and Lyman families. While donations of artifacts continued strong, cash contributions were meager. The number of visitors increased each year, and teachers brought their classes to visit and learn. Always willing to help, Levi and Nettie often gave special presentations.

As the third-generation Lymans grew older, the torch was passed. Ellen died in 1940, but Nettie and Levi continued to work at the Museum during the war years.

In November 1947, Nettie died, soon after she and Levi celebrated their 50th anniversary. Less than a year later, Levi followed her. Like his father and mother before him—and his grandfather and grandmother before that—Levi and his wife spent their lives contributing to the education of Hilo and Hawaiʻi Island.

Into the 1970s, these specially converted passenger cars called "Hilo Sampans" were used as taxicabs in Hilo. Museum director Dr. Leon Bruno, behind the wheel, scrounged up and carefully restored several of them, to return some color (and practicality) to Hilo's streets.

The staff of Lyman House Memorial Museum. Front: Lynn Manuel and Dr. Leon Bruno. Second row: Brigitte Mattos, Linda Collazo and Mary Callahan. Third row: Esther Meyers, Charlene Dahlquist, Wes Awana, Daisy Bergen and Gloria Kobayashi. Back row: Samson Kela, Kathleen Adams, Georgia Salcedo and Paul Dahlquist.

The seeds of community service planted by David and Sarah continued to flourish.

And the Museum continued to flourish as well. For some forty years, it served as a general repository, displaying everything from Hawaiian artifacts to shell collections and Mission items. It was also the setting for educational and cultural gatherings for community groups.

In the late 1960s, Orlando Lyman, Levi's son (and David and Sarah's great-grandson), envisioned a major expansion. He had constructed a modern, three-story building, next to the Mission House, to display, among other things, his collec-tion of minerals from around the world.

In the planning stages, Orlando and his wife Helen visited over 70 museums in the United States and Canada, to gather ideas for displays and exhibits. Once this new building opened in 1972, the exhibits in the original Mission House were rearranged to depict the living quarters of David and Sarah Lyman and their family. Many original pieces of furniture and other period items were located, and today a visitor can step back into 19th century Hilo.

A major restoration was undertaken on the Mission House in 1982 for the sesquicentennial celebration of the arrival of the missionary Lymans. Recent efforts focus on interpreting the house and its contents as it most probably looked in the late 1860s, during the latter years of the Lymans' ministry in Hilo.

As this is written in 1992, two rooms display *koa* furniture, some of it of a very unique design, built by HBS students in the late 19th and early 20th centuries. This is a fitting tribute to the pioneering efforts of David Lyman as founder and teacher of the School.

The Lyman House Memorial Museum was established to provide the community with a link to its past, "to tell the story of Hawai'i, its islands and its people." It is dedicated to providing future generations with a place to collect, preserve and protect aspects of history in the making.

During the early years, there was a concerted effort to locate, preserve and exhibit Lyman family items, as well as artifacts of Hawai'i's culture worthy of museum display. The new building permits a major expansion of that effort.

The Museum's ground floor houses a Special Exhibits Gallery where traveling, internally-generated and community-originated exhibits are shown on a rotating basis. This area is also used for workshops, lectures and classes. The first floor holds a book and gift shop and the Island Heritage Gallery, with exhibits of seven of the major immigrant groups—Hawaiian, Japanese, Chinese, Caucasian, Filipino, Portuguese and Korean. The second floor's Earth Heritage Gallery displays Orlando's mineral collection, rated as one of the best in the U.S., as well as a world-class seashell collection.

An outstanding Hawai'i Volcano exhibit and a new display on Astronomy—the only one of its kind in the State—fill out the Gallery. The second floor also has a small gallery of Chinese Art and another featuring Hawaiian Artists—all part of the Museum's permanent collections. Today there is a renewed effort to acquire additional items for all departments to enhance and improve the Museum's displays and offerings to the public.

Although not in the original plans, a major collection of Hawaiiana—print and photographs—has emerged, creating a rich lode for researchers as well as the community in general.

A small but very highly-motivated professional staff is assisted by a large cadre of volunteers to perform services

Visitors to the Museum listen attentively as an interpreter discusses Hawai'i's volcanos.

not only needed to maintain the basic purpose of the Museum but to respond to an increasing number of requests for assistance from the entire community. The Museum is no longer only a place for visitors to browse on a rainy day or for residents to bring guests on occasion. It is

an important component of the Hilo community, linking the business and educational sectors, among others.

Even a casual observer is soon aware that, aside from the fine artifacts and exhibits, the educational program is the strongest of all the Museum's offerings. At the same time the professional museum community nationwide was emphasizing the educational responsibilities of its members, the Lyman Museum was hard at work developing comprehensive programs and curriculum. Visits by school groups had always been emphasized, even soon after the Museum opened in 1931. The Trustees envisioned a more active role for the Museum in fulfilling its obligation to provide resources for students.

Since 1982, there has been a concerted effort to create a curriculum of Early Hawaiian Culture through a series of workshops developed and conducted

Left to right: Museum director Leon Bruno and Trustees Fred Koehnen, Bill Thibadeau, Hugh Willocks, Buddy Gordon, Alice Fujimoto, Donn Carlsmith, Richard Penhallow, Roy Blackshear, June Hitchcock Humme and Richard Henderson.

by Museum staff. These are regularly scheduled in classrooms throughout the Island of Hawai'i with written materials and video tapes available for schools and groups beyond. These workshops are also well received by visitors in the Elder-hostel program sponsored by the Museum.

As a result of its growing reputation for providing learning experiences of things Hawaiian, the Museum was approached during the summer of 1988 to determine its interest in becoming a site for the rapidly growing International Elderhostel Program. Commencing in January 1989, the Museum has become one of a small handful of non-academic institutions successfully offering this week-long educational program to an ever-expanding audience. One of the strongest features is the opportunity for the participants to gain an in-depth knowledge about topics the casual visitor to the Museum can never obtain. Perhaps this gives added impetus to the present-day missionary role as defined in its mission statement "to tell the story of

Hawai'i, its islands and its people."

Lyman House Memorial Museum was accredited by the American Association of Museums in 1972, re-accredited in 1983, it will soon be time (in 1993) for the Museum to once again demonstrate to the profession and the community its continuing growth, looking to the future for even greater service to the com-munity—a tradition long associated with the Lyman legacy.

The Museum's economic health clearly indicates the strong financial support which has been received and is steadily growing from both the general public and the business community, not only in Hilo but throughout the State. To sustain that support is probably the greatest challenge facing the Trustees, staff and volunteers.

The quality and the success of the Museum is a fitting tribute to a family which has given their commitment, their talents and their energies to the Hilo Mission, Hilo Boarding School and the Lyman House Memorial Museum.

Orlando Lyman...
Continuing his Family's Tradition

Sarah and David Lyman's great-grandson, Orlando, was born in the HBS principal's house on November 19, 1903 and lived there with his parents, Levi and Nettie, and his older sister, Kathryn. He took an early interest

Orlando's birthplace, the principal's house at HBS, is shown in this view, which was taken a few years before he was born.

in the School farm, as HBS was a virtual experimental station, testing new varieties of garden crops and discarding those that did poorly. Orlando was fascinated by plants.

Orlando was always curious, and he recalled encountering snow during the family's mainland trip in 1917-18. While his parents were visiting the White House, it began to snow, and Orlando, then 12, was fascinated by the falling crystals. He had opened the window to examine them more closely, when his mother arrived home and put a stop to this natural history lesson, for she did not

appreciate the wet spots left behind nor the cold air pouring into the room. But the beauty and structure of the flakes enchanted Orlando, who later devoted much of his life to collecting and studying mineral crystals and specimens.

He attended Hilo Union Elementary, then Hilo High, after two years, Punahou in Honolulu where his father, grandfather and many uncles, aunts and cousins had gone. An outstanding student, Orlando was valedictorian of his class.

Orlando learned of sugar production on a small homestead plantation of Levi's in Kaūmana, and he decided to make it his career. He first went to the University of Hawai'i to study sugar technology, then the Massachusetts Agricultural College (now UMass) for two years, including a summer course in business administration at Columbia University. Orlando spent his senior year back at UH to prepare for a career in Hawai'i's sugar industry.

Since any change on a plantation impacted all other operations, students learned every detail of plantation life— from the jobs in the canefields and in the sugar mills, right on up to the manager's office itself. After he graduated in 1927, Orlando was hired by the Hawai'i Sugar Planters' Association (HSPA) and was assigned to the Maui Experiment Station.

His task was to develop new varieties of sugar cane through hybridization and cross-pollination. This was a delicate operation for the flowers are tiny, and miniscule pollen grains were spread on black paper, then carefully transferred to the healthiest-looking flowers. Later, ripe seeds gathered from the "mother" tassels, were germinated and grown in containers. A very few were promoted to test plots where they were studied for high sugar contact, resistance to wind, drought, diseases, excessive tasseling, and an ability to "close in" quickly (to shade out weeds). Finally, the most promising were selected for field trials, and the winners replaced inferior varieties at the next planting. Orlando was very good at this work and spent most of his career on plantations testing new varieties of cane.

Orlando worked on other projects to save time and money, such as eliminating planting cane in hills like corn, and the use of a ratoon crop. At this time fields were cleared after early summer harvest, and they lay fallow, during the best growing season, until winter planting. Orlando and the HSPA team felt that yield could be increased by developing a ratoon crop from the old clumps. Test plots succeeded beyond their wildest expectations.

Proper soil nutrient balances were especially tricky on Maui, where the fertile central plain had been covered by the ocean in the fairly recent geologic past. The soil there had more calcium (from coral and shells) than *ma uka* fields.

Orlando took occasional trips home to Hilo, and there met Helen Maxson, executive secretary of the YWCA. Born on a small Iowa farm in Iowa, where her family raised fruits, vegetables and livestock, Helen graduated from Iowa State Teachers' College with a major in Latin. There were, she soon discovered, precious few opportunities for Latin teachers, and she moved to Hilo with the YWCA in 1929.

Helen and Orlando were married in Hilo on June 24, 1933, and moved into a cottage on Maui. Three years later, they were transferred to Hawai'i, when the HSPA felt the Experiment Station's work on Maui had become routine.

At that time, the Island of Hawai'i produced nearly a third of the Territory's sugar—and had over 100,000 acres in cultivation. Because of the Island's extreme diversity, Orlando and the researchers had their work cut out.

Soil testing was a first priority, for soils that were almost chemically identical produced widely different rates of growth—depending on their depth, the climate, available water, and the elevation. Rainy North Hilo slopes lost fertility rapidly from the run-off of heavy downpours. Irrigated North Kohala fields

Orlando Hammond Lyman with his mother, Nettie, and his older sister, Kathryn.

suffered from wind damage and dry air.

There was resistance from many old-time plantation people to the HSPA suggestions, especially replacing their traditional favorite, Yellow Caledonia, with newer varieties. Gradually new ideas were accepted, especially those which cut labor costs and increased yields.

World War II brought problems. Neither laborers nor machines could work at night since Hawai'i was under a strict black-out. Adequate fertilizer was hard to get, because it used nitrogen also needed for gunpowder and explosives. Labor was in short supply. Teenagers were excused from school one day a week to work in the fields, with teachers as overseers.

Increased airplane traffic between Hawai'i and the South Pacific, the Philippines and other areas where sugar grew, brought new insects and diseases. This was especially when troops came back from the front for R&R, because there was no time to thoroughly disinfect planes, and insect eggs and disease spores are not easy to find. Military authorities were more concerned with the possible introduction of human diseases like malaria than with those affecting sugar.

Efforts to control these new insects and diseases by traditional means were not very successful. Orlando felt that new "blood lines" of resistant sugar cane must be developed. The process was a slow,

Orlando Lyman at work on one of his life's passions—the study of minerals. Hawai'i Island is a fascinating place to start such a collection, because of the varied colors of sand beaches and the many different types of lava. Orlando's collection, however, spanned the globe.

expensive one, and biological controls gave way to chemical sprays that were faster and more thorough. By then, however, Orlando had perfected disease resistant strains for use in hybrids, which proved successful.

Agriculture is a constant battle—as fast as one problem is solved—or at least partially solved—another arises. Some varieties produced fine big flower tassels, but all at the same time, at the peak of the plants' production of sugar, which declined quickly after flowering. It was impossible for field crews and mills to process all this cane at once, so Orlando and his team set to work breeding cane that would allow a longer harvesting period without losing sugar content.

The unionization of plantation labor increased rapidly after World War II, and plantations countered with increased mechanization and a smaller labor force, to which they could then afford to give higher wages. Orlando continued working on problems relating to both the cane itself and mechanization in the fields.

When he returned to Hawai'i Island in 1936, old-fashioned methods and cane varieties were still in use, and a large labor force produced an average yield per acre of just three to six tons. Erosion, loss of soil fertility, weed growth, and other difficulties plagued plantations. By the time Orlando retired thirty-one years later, the average annual yield had increased to more than ten tons per acre, produced by a much smaller crew.

Although he had retired from the sugar industry, he remained active in local business and community affairs including, of course, the Museum. Like his father

Visitors to the Lyman Museum enjoy the spectacular mineral exhibit in the Earth Heritage Gallery.

and grandfather before him, Orlando served as a director on many boards, including Hilo Electric Light, Hilo Gas Co, Realty Investment, First Trust Company, Hilo Motors, Hilo Yacht Club and the Rotary Club of Hilo.

Orlando was long active in the church and just as Levi had taken over the church duties and management of Homelani Cemetery when his father Fred could no longer carry them on, Orlando did the same for his father. He also served on the board of trustees of Hilo Boarding School and, with Helen, of the Lyman House Memorial Museum.

After a distinguished career in sugar, and a lifetime of community service, Orlando Lyman died in 1986 at the age of 83. His widow Helen died in 1990. Their generosity is responsible for publication of this book.

THE CREATION OF THIS BOOK...

THE BACKGROUND:

The Lymans of Hawai'i Island, A Pioneering Family came about through a bequest from Orlando Lyman, who started the project some years ago when he hired Helen Baldwin to research his family history. She laboriously studied and transcribed scratchy journals and yellowing letters in the Lyman Archives. The thrifty Yankees often wrote letters in miniscule cursive, with no margins. Then they'd turn the sheet 90° and continue, writing right over their original words. Reading these letters in 1840 must have been quite a task— reading them after more than a century of fading, as Helen did, must have been grinding drudgery. Her efforts resulted in a manuscript packed with invaluable research.

Helen Spivey Baldwin in 1970

The first step was to enter all of Mrs. Baldwin's work into the Macintosh. I tried to scan the pages in, then "read" them with a special OCR (optical character recognition) program—to little avail. It worked, sort of, but had the twin distinctions of being interminably slow *and* inaccurate.

I then started entering the material by hand, but three days (and nine pages) later, realized that it would have to be transcribed by someone who did not "type" with two fingers while staring mesmerizied at the keyboard, searching for each letter. My speed is measured not in words-per-minute, but rather characters-per-hour. I called Bonnie Scannel, an old friend and great typist, who soon pounded every word flawlessly into the HD-20 drive on my old Mac Plus.

Once Mrs. Baldwin's research was in the Mac, the task of actually planning and writing the book came into play. This was, without question, the toughest project I've ever tackled. After two complete re-writes—and halfway through a third—I stepped away for a time to analyze the direction the book needed to take. The story was far less one of individual Lymans, I finally realized, than that of a family with a century and a half tradition of service to Hilo.

First, of course, was the Hilo Mission, where David and Sarah provided a stabilizing influence after a succession of missionaries had moved in, and out. Next, Hilo Boarding School, with its huge impact on Hawaiians—and later peoples of the Pacific—for a century. Throughout, HBS was imprinted by one Lyman or another. Third, was the Lyman House Memorial Museum, started by the family to save the old homestead from destruction. Over almost sixty years, it has evolved into a world-class, fully-accredited institution.

The realization that the family's contributions were the theme of the book meant an extremely complex fourth re-write, and later a fifth. But the effort was immaterial, for at last I had the key.

A DOCTOR OF WORDS

Toward the end of the project, as terror set in, I called Paul Berry, alias Doc, a Punahou teacher and a terrific editor. His job, I said, as I handed him ten disks and a machete, was to trim the excesses that I had wrought. He gave me four disks back, and suggested many transitions and conclusions. As a lifelong educator, Doc had an empathy for HBS that shines through.

THE MACINTOSH:

This project could not have been done—at least by me—without the Macintosh. The Mac is, as David Belden Lyman might have said, a "godsend." It asks for little else but 120 volts and good software. I have been tapping consonants and the occasional vowel into one since 1986, including writing a best-seller (*WhaleSong*) and doing most of the research and copy for Hawai'i Maritime Center. Yet I still don't have a clue about computers. Bits, bytes, ROM, RAM and clock speed—I've heard all the buzz words, but I take a perverse pride in not knowing what any of 'em mean. The Macintosh does not require me to know and so I don't. It is an almost transparent platform for creativity.

For those who are interested, this book was produced on four computers: my elderly Mac Plus and HD-20 drive; a nifty little Powerbook 100; a Mac IIci and 19" Radius color monitor, and a Mac SE with a Radius full-page display. The type was run out on a 600 dpi Apple LaserWriter Pro 630. All performed flawlessly.

Software was—as is my practice—very limited: original files were typed into Word 4.0 and then imported and manipulated in QuarkXpress 3.1 on Apple's "old" System 6.07. My philosophy is to let others try new stuff as it comes out, so I can experience incompatabilities vicariously.

All the book files, chapters, graphics, notes, etc. were continuously backed up on **three** complete sets of floppies. Scanning for placement was on an HP ScanJet Plus, perhaps the easiest piece of complex equipment I've ever used.

A DESIGNER EXTRAORDINAIRE

I served as my own designer—and a great one, too— UNTIL the moment that I looked at the finished product without rose-colored glasses, and realized that while no one would ever shout, "It's awful!" neither would they shout, "It's wonderful!" So I called up a real pro, award-winning graphic designer Malinda Abell, whose talent and taste make these pages what they are. Malinda did a complete make-over, adding "air" (white space) and far better flow.

COLOR, COLOR, COLOR

I elected to shoot every image in color, even though the vast majority were originally monochrome. A look at the Obookiah frontispiece on page 14, David's journal on 30 or the Coan portrait on page 46 will demonstrate why. Color brings out subtleties and nuances of age that are lost with black and white film. Luckily, on the advice of Leon Bruno at LHMM, we used a photographer from Hilo who—working only from a faxxed list—did consistently fine work. Old documents, artifacts, groups, interiors, exteriors, studio work, Mark Watanabe shot it all—and shot it beautifully. In Honolulu, an old friend from *WhaleSong*, Bob Chinn, did his usual excellent job as we tramped from one archives to another to shoot. Both are tremendous photographers and were a special joy to work with.

We actually scanned and placed the images two different ways. Some were done "traditionally" in Hong Kong, while others were scanned into the Mac on a Howtek D-4000 drum scanner, separated in Adobe Photoshop and checked on a 3M Rainbow Color Proofer. For this end of the project, I was extremely lucky to work with Kelly Ann Fukuhara, who is both a great designer AND a techie.

A SPECIAL PAINTING:

The painting on page 16 is a story in itself. The book needed color early on, and I called an old friend, Gary Reed, to do a picture of David and Sarah leaving her Vermont farmhouse after their wedding. It seemed easy...until Gary started asking questions. What did the house look like? What was the lay of the land? What about the stagecoach? What style clothing were the people wearing? Was the moon out?

My first call was to the town clerk of Royalton, Vermont, who gave me John Dumville's number. It may have been the most important phone number in the project, for John—a historian for the state and for Royalton as well—couldn't have been more helpful. He did legwork, research, xeroxing and pointed me towards one expert after another. His contribution is an integral part of much of the first couple of chapters—especially Gary's painting.

I finally got to meet John Dumville in May 1991 when I drove over to Royalton on a rainy Sunday, and we "jeeped" up the old County Road to the Joiner's cellarhole. The abandoned farmhouse had burned down after a lightning strike in the 1940s, and the lush pastures, so laboriously cleared by hand and oxen a couple of hundred years ago, had long since been reclaimed by the second-growth maples and birches. But the visit did net me the "lay of the land" for Gary. I knew now the house was on a rise and where the stagecoach would have stopped to load the young couple.

The other questions? John came up with a photo of the house. He pointed me to a Vermont judge and expert on period clothing, Merideth Wright, who sent off sketches of shapes and details. He filled in the blanks on the stagecoach. The last detail was the moon. I hoped against hope that it was a dramatic, luminous full moon, suspended softly over the snow-clad hills. I called the Astronomy Department at UH, and they ran November 3, 1831, at 2 AM, in Royalton, Vermont through some esoteric Macintosh software and determined there was no moon at all that night. Oh, well.

Finally, we had all the pieces. Gary took them to his Maile studio and came up with a suitably cold, somber picture—the newlyweds were, after all, leaving family and friends behind forever on a cold winter night.

AN ELUSIVE IMAGE:

A great deal of time on a historical project of this magnitude is devoted to research and sourcing. With a lot of help, I tracked down image after image, but there was one I kept missing. Much of my fascination with history stems from my childhood in a 1791 farmhouse in rural northern New Jersey. Growing up in the country gave me a love of old lithographs of farm scenes from the 18th and 19th centuries.

I needed an image to illustrate a farm being created from primeval forest, and remembered an old print showing trees being girdled and felled, and stumps being extracted by a yoke of oxen. But I couldn't find the print—anywhere. I pored over my books, hit the libraries, and even started calling dealers, experts and museums in the Northeast.

I was beginning to think I'd just conjured the whole thing up, and was searching not for an image, but for an imaginary one. Finally, a call paid off, to *Yankee* magazine, the journal of New England, asking if perhaps anyone on the staff remembered such a picture. Eight months later came the answer—not only did someone remember it, but they had an original they'd sell. For $16! I then called Honolulu artist/photographer Lani Yamasaki to see if she could add some subtle color. Mark photographed the original, and Lani tinted the print. The resulting image is on page 22.

MORE MAC PEOPLE:

Over the course of the last eight years, I have probably averaged ten hours a day, seven days a week, on the Macintosh. I have found Mac people to be universally generous with their time, their expertise and their friendship. Somehow, it's not just a computer, it's a community!

My publisher/collaborator on *WhaleSong*, Bob Goodman, was—as always—generous with help. He was just finishing *In the Wake of Dreams, Reflections of Hawai'i* by Doc Berry as I was finishing this book, so we have been running parallel paths for much of the past year. His path—testing the newest programs and equipment—is a lot steeper than mine, and his bold and brilliant work has put him on the cutting-edge of Macintosh technology. All of us doing desktop publishing owe a debt to the creators of the Macintosh and a second debt to Bob Goodman. Thanks, my friend.

The phone has been a constant companion in this project, calling Hilo and New England and especially calling Ken Kimura, my Macintosh oracle. When it comes to computers, I am like the infamous lady who takes her car to the mechanic and says, "It goes 'boinkity-boink' sometimes." My descriptions are imprecise and occasionally silly. Ken will interpret my frantic gibberish and then explain exactly what to do—often at outrageous hours of the night.

UH Poly Sci prof Doug Bwy has also always been ready to help with technical advice, as has Rolf Nordahl of MacMouse Club. Gordon Santiago of LithoPhoto was absolutely invaluable during scanning. Artist/publisher (and Salerno's lunchmate) Don Hardy pointed me in the right direction for printing in Hong Kong. And my special thanks to Mike Klein, who has probably helped more people with computers over the years than anyone in Hawai'i.

THE EARLY BELIEFS:

Perhaps the most intensive research on my part went into an area which only occupies a very few pages in the book, namely where—religiously—the ABCFM missionaries were coming from. I learned early on that the religious freedom established in New England helped create and maintain the American Revolution, something I had never heard before in years of history classes. I learned that Yale was founded as a reaction to Harvard becoming too "liberal." And that David's alma mater, Andover Theological Seminary, was formed when Yale itself became too liberal.

Over the years I had heard Hawai'i's missionaries called Calvinists (almost always modified by *stern*), Presbyterians, Congregationalists...all different Protestant sects. Although the ABCFM was founded by Congregationalists, they accepted other denominations as well, so the missionaries to Hawai'i were indeed of mixed denominations.

Most of them—in the first few years especially—were a pretty conservative lot. They reflected the hardscabble values of New Englanders of the time, values they saw as necessary for survival in a tough world. They were at odds with the Hawaiians, who after all lived in a less physically challenging land. A place like Vermont had long, terrible winters, lousy soil and a short growing season. The people there were an especially Spartan lot. Hawai'i had no winter and a year-round growing season. New England's mores were, in most ways, a difficult (and poor) fit.

I was especially intrigued by the severe limitations placed on Hawaiian church membership by these early men of the cloth, who, after all, had come some 18,000 miles with the express purpose of converting heathens to Christ. Except for the ali'i—whose support the missionaries desperately needed—so few Hawaiians were permitted to join that the church was almost an exclusive club. The missionaries applied the same stringent requirements that they themselves had met, requirements like the so-called "adult experience" or vision of God. This was not easy for the Hawaiians, apparently, and miniscule numbers were baptized. Later, during the Great Revival, all this went out the window, and baptisms were performed by the thousands in a single day.

I was not—am not—a big fan of missionaries of any stripe, because I have a philosophical bent against people going off and telling other people what to believe and how to act. Yet through their words and thoughts and deeds, I came to know and like David and Sarah Lyman immensely. They were humble, hard-working, simple, committed people, whose minds seemed to become more and more open the longer they stayed in the Islands. While some ABCFM people displayed what appear to be enormous egos, dunderheaded (perhaps even evil) manipulation of history and the Hawaiians, and self-serving behavior, the quiet, decent Lymans lived out their lives of service in Hilo.

OTHER LYMANS:

David and Sarah arrived in these Islands almost precisely 160 years before these words are being written. Seven of their eight children lived to adulthood and sired forty third-generation grandchildren, who in turn...well, you get the idea—there have been literally several hundred Lymans descended from David and Sarah, many of them prominent citizens of the Islands, and a few of them my good friends. Lyman scions have been or are harbor masters, sea captains, Bishop Estate trustees, schoolteachers, Hokule'a crewmembers and business, church and community leaders.

Since this book focused on the Mission, Hilo Boarding School and the Lyman Museum, it necessarily focuses on those Lymans whose roots were close to Hilo and who were involved specifically in those endeavors—hence the almost lineal fix on David and Sarah, Fred and Bella, Levi and Nettie, Ellen, and Orlando.

ACKNOWLEDGEMENTS:

First, and foremost, Dr. Leon Bruno, director of the Lyman Museum. Leon selected me for the project and stood by me as the time passed and the book *slowly* evolved. It was a convoluted process, and Leon was understanding, supportive and extremely helpful. He also helped "proof" the book—a terminally thankless task—and wrote much of the Museum copy in Chapter 8. Leon is also a first-cabin museum director and contributor to Hilo.

Leon was joined on the Book Committee by trustees Tina Whitmarsh (a Lyman descendant) and Roy Blackshear (of the missionary Shipman family), and both offered helpful critiques and corrections.

The LHMM registrar, Lynn Manuel, deserves a chapter, instead of a paragraph. Her initiative, suggestions, follow-through and enthusiasm were all an enormous boon. She tirelessly tracked down artifacts and images, and because most photography had to be done after-hours, she stayed late to help. Lynn is the unsung heroine of this book, because unlike the rest of us, you can't "see" what she did. Suffice to say, her contribution was immense. *Mahalo nui*, Lynn.

The Library & Archives at LHMM just keep getting better and better! Materials are now computerized, cross-referenced and infinitely easier to find. Librarians Gloria Kobayashi and Charlene Dahlquist were extremely helpful searching through original source documents and materials and making suggestions.

Author (and former LHMM trustee) June Hitchcock Humme sourced family photos and images and made many valuable suggestions which ended up in the finished product. LHMM Board president Richard Henderson offered great insights into Hilo's economic growth, and retired sugar exec Wakey Mist detailed Orlando's contribution to the sugar industry and Hilo.

Honolulu harbor pilot (and fellow denizen of Aloha Tower), Capt. David B.K. Lyman IV, told me of David's Hawaiian citizenship (pages 54-5). Another descendant, Rufus' great-great-grandson, Bruce Lambert, gave me some invaluable info on Rufus, including his award of the Order of Kamehameha I from King Kalākaua (72-3).

Honolulu's great repository of ABCFM missionary ephemera is the Mission Houses Museum Library. I began working there with librarian Mary Jane Knight, until one day I saw her behind the desk at my favorite public library in Ka'imukī. Luckily, she was replaced by an equally great librarian, Marilyn Reppuhn, ably assisted by Judy Kearney. Barbara Dunn of the Hawaii Historical Society, which shares space in the Mission House Library, was also a huge help.

Many others contributed as well. The town historian of Cornwall, CT, Michael Gannett, went out in a snowstorm with a flashlight and a broom to get an accurate transcription of Henry Obookiah's headstone. Researcher Belinda Nettles dredged the Archives for material. Noted Pacific historian Rhoda Hackler shared her research on the early missionaries. Linguist and author Ruby Johnson helped me understand traditional Hawaiian beliefs, and UH Hawaiian instructor Puakea Nogelmeier read the copy over twice and offered correct translations, usage and punctuation.

Artist and *Hōkūle'a* crewman Wainwright Piena let us use his petroglyph canoe (page 9), designer Kalani Ogata re-drew the HBS logo, and Katie Doka did the "family tree" on pages 62-3. Rick Ralston of Crazy Shirts and the Lahaina Whaling Museum okayed use of rare whaling images from his extensive collection. Hawai'i's famed artist/historian Herb Kāne (whose father attended HBS) allowed us to use two of his paintings and shared some great stories about the School.

Thank you one and all!

Bibliography

LYMAN FAMILY & HILO BOARDING SCHOOL
Gen. S. C. Armstrong, *A Successful Piece of Missionary Work* in Jubilee Notes (50th Anniversary of HBS) 1886

E. M. Damon & Kathryn L. Bond, *David Belden Lyman, Sarah Joiner Lyman, 1832-1932*, brochure written for centennial celebration, E. M. Damon, LHMM

M. O. Gordon, *History of the Hilo Boarding School*, manusript copy at LHMM

HBS Scrapbook, Vol. I and II (at LHMM)

David B. Lyman, *Station Letters, David Belden Lyman to Levi Chamberlain*, bound manuscript (at LHMM)

Ellen G. Lyman & Elsie H. Wilcox, *David Belden Lyman and Sarah Joiner Lyman, A Geneology of Their Family in Hawaii, 1832-1933*, HI, private printing, 1933

Henry M. Lyman, *Hawaiian Yesterdays*, IL, A.C. McClerg, 1906

Nettie H. Lyman, *History of Haili Church, 1824-1942*, HI, private printing, 1942

Nettie H. Lyman, ed, *Notes on the Hilo Boarding School, 1836-1936*, bound manuscript (at LHMM)

Sarah J. Lyman, *Letters from Sarah Joiner Lyman to Melissa Joiner Hall, 1833-1883*, bound manuscript, (at LHMM)

Sarah J. Lyman, *The Earthquake Book*, bound note-book (original), in LHMM, first entry is dated Oct. 3, 1833

Margaret Greer Martin, ed, *The Lymans of Hilo*, (journal and letters of Sarah Lyman, with add'l essays). HI, LHMM, 1979

OTHER EARLY MISSIONARIES IN HAWAI'I
Mary Charlotte Alexander, ed, *Dr. Baldwin of Lahaina*, CA, Stanford U. Press, 1953

Rufus Anderson, *The Hawaiian Islands, Their Progress and Condition Under Missionary Labors*, MA, Gould and Lincoln, 1865

Rev. Hiram Bingham, *A Residence of 21 Years in the Sandwich Islands*, NY, Praefer Publishers, 1969. (FP in 1847)

Rev. Titus Coan, *Life in Hawaii*, NY, Anson D. F. Randolph and Co., 1882

Ethel M. Damon, ed, *Letters From the Life of Abner and Lucy Wilcox, 1836-1869*, HI, private printing, 1950

Emma Lyons Doyle, ed, *Makua Laina, the Story of Lorenzo Lyons*, HI, Advertiser Publishing Co., 1935

William Ellis, *Journal of William Ellis, Narrative of a Tour of Owhyhee*, VT, Charles E. Tuttle & Co, 1979 (FP in 1825)

Rev. Ephraim Eveleth, *History of the Sandwich Islands, With An Account of the Mission*, PA, Am. Sunday School Union, 1840

Mary Dillingham Frear, *Lowell and Abigail*, CT, private printing, 1934

Walter F. Frear, *Anti-Missionary Criticism with Reference to Hawaii*, HI, Advertiser Publishing Co, 1935

Patricia Grimshaw, *Paths of Duty, American Missionary Wives in Nineteenth-Century Hawaii*, HI, UH Press, 1989

Frances J. Halford, *Nine Doctors and God*, HI, UH Press, 1954

Jean Hobbs, *Hawaii, A Pageant of the Soil*, CA, Stanford Press, 1935

Audrey B. Sexton & Album Committee, *Missionary Album, Sesquicentennial Edition*, HI, Edward Enterprises, Inc. 1969

Lucy G. Thurston, *Life and Times of Mrs. Lucy G. Thurston*, MI, S. C. Andrews, 1882

C. S. Stewart, *Journal of a Residence in the Sandwich Islands*, HI, UH Press, 1970 (FP in 1827)

EARLY NEW ENGLAND & MISSIONARY MOVEMENT
Bertha S. Dodge, *Vermont By Choice, The Earliest Years*, VT, The New England Press, 1987

Edwin Dwight, ed, *Memoirs of Henry Obookiah*, HI, Woman's Board of Missions for Pacific Islands, United Church of Christ, 150th anniversary edition, 1968 (FP in 1818)

Alice Morse Earle, *Customs and Fashions in Old New England*, VT, Charles E. Tuttle Company, 1988 (FP in 1893)

William R. Hutchinson, *Errand to the World, American Protestant Thought and Foreign Missions*, U of Chicago Press, IL, 1987

Donna-Belle Garvin & James L. Garvin, *On the Road North of Boston*, New Hampshire Historical Society, NH, 1988

Kenneth A. Lockridge, *Literacy in Colonial New England*, NY, Norton & Company, 1974

David S. Lovejoy, *The Glorious Revolution in America*, CT, Wesleyan U Press, 1987

Evelyn Wood Lovejoy, ed, *History of Royalton, Vol I*, VT, Published by the town and the Royalton Woman's Club, 1911

Hope Nash, *Royalton, Vermont*, VT, Published by the town, the Royalton Woman's Club and the Historical Society, 1975

New England (essays originally published in Harper's Magazine in late 1800s) NY, Gallery Books, 1990

Rowland E. Robinson, *Vermont, A Study of Independence*, VT, Tuttle, 1975 (FP in 1892)

EARLY DAYS IN HAWAI'I
Isabella L. Bird, *Six Months in the Sandwich Islands*, HI, UH Press, 1964 (FP in 1875)

Peter H. Buck, *Arts and Crafts of Hawaii*, HI, Bishop Museum Press, 1957

Robert Dampier, *To the Sandwich Islands on H.M.S. Blonde*, HI, U.H. Press, 1971 (FP in 1826)

A. Grove Day, ed. *Mark Twain's Letters from Hawaii*, HI, UH Press, 1971

David Douglas (from 1833-4 journal by W. F. Wilson), *David Douglas, Botanist at Hawaii*, HI, New Freedom Press, 1919

Nathaniel B. Emerson, *Unwritten Literature of Hawaii*, DC, Government Press, 1909

David W. Forbes & Thomas K. Kunchika, *Hilo, 1825-1925, A Century of Paintings and Drawings*, HI, LHMM, 1983

Milton C. George, *The Development of Hilo, Hawaii, T. H.*, MI, The Edwards Letter Shop, 1948

E. S. Craighill Handy & Mary Kawena Pūku'i, *Polynesian Family System in Ka'u,Hawaii*, VT, Tuttle & Co, 1972

Hawaiian Historical Society Annual Reports, 1909/10/12/15

Hilo Tribune Herald. April 9, 1943 Supplement, titled *History of the First Foreign Church and Society of Hilo*, at LHMM

Honolulu Star-Bulletin, (unsigned), *Men of Hawaii*, Vol. IV

Herb Kawainui Kāne, *Voyagers*, WA, WhaleSong, Inc, Beyond Words Pub., 1991

Melvin Lord & J.C. Holbrook, *Juvenile Lyre*, MA, Richardson, Lord and Holbrook, 1831 (later translated into Hawaiian)

James Macrae, *With Lord Byron at the Sandwich Islands in 1825*, HI, reprinted by Petroglyph Press, 1972

David Malo, *Hawaiian Antiquities*, HI, Bishop Museum Press, 1951 reprint of 1898 translation (FP in Hawaiian in 1839)

Francis Allyn Olmsted, *Incidents of a Whaling Voyage*, VT, Tuttle & Co., 1969 (FP in 1841)

Stanley D. Porteus, *Calabashes and Kings*, London, George G. Harrap & Co, 1954

Helen H. Roberts, *Ancient Hawaiian Music*, HI, Bishop Museum Press, 1926

Thomas G. Thrum, *The Centennial Book, 100 Years of Christian Civilization in Hawaii*, HI, Central Committee of Hawaiian Mission Centennial, 1920

Herman J. Viola & Carolyn Margolis, ed., *Magnificent Voyagers, The U.S. Exploring Expedition 1838-1842*, DC, Smithsonian Institution Press, 1985

Derek Wilson, *The Circumnavigators*, NY, Evans & Co, 1989

Kristin Zambucka, *Kalākaua, Hawaii's Last King*, HI, Mana Publishing Co., 1983

EARLY PROTESTANT RELIGIOUS BELIEFS
John A. Andrew III, *Rebuilding the Christian Commonwealth: New England Congregationalists & Foreign Missions, 1800-1830*, KY, U. of Kentucky Press, 1976

Patricia Bonomi, *Under the Cope of Heaven: Religion, Society and Politics in Colonial America*, NY, Oxford U. Press, 1986

David D. Hall, *Worlds of Wonder, Days of Judgement, Popular Religious Belief in Early New England*, NY, Alfred A. Knopf, 1989

W.R. Hutchison, *Errand to the World: American Protestant Thought and Foreign Missions*, IL, U. of Chicago Press, 1987

David S. Lovejoy, *Religious Enthusiasm in the New World, Heresy to Revolution*, MA, Harvard U. Press, 1985

Cotton Mather, *Cotton Mather on Witchcraft*, NY, Dorset Press 1991, (FP in 1692)

W.G. McLoughlin, ed, *The American Evangelicals, 1800-1900, An Anthology*, MA, Peter Smith, 1976

Harry S. Stout, *The New England Soul, Preaching and Religious Culture in Colonial New England*, NY, Oxford U. Press, 1986

James C. Thomson Jr, *A Cycle of Cathay*, in American Heritage, Vol 23, No. 5, Aug. 1972

EARTH SCIENCE
J. D. Dana, *History of Changes in Kilauea*, in *American Journal of Science*, Vol. 35, April, 1888

J.D. Dana, *History of Changes in the Mt. Loa Craters*, American Journal of Science, Vol. 24 June, 1887/Vol. 36, July 1888

George C. Daniels, ed, *Earthquake*, NY, Time-Life Books,1982

George C. Daniels, ed, *Volcano*, NY, Time-Life Books,1982

Jean McKean Grace, ed, *Marine Atlas of Hawaii, Bays & Harbors*, HI, Sea Grant, 1974

A.L. Hammond, *Dilatancy: Growing Acceptance as an Earthquake Mechanism*, Science, May 3, 1974

Charles H. Hitchcock, *Hawaii and its Volcanoes*, HI, The Hawaiian Gazette Co., 1909

J. H. Whitcomb, J. E. Garmany, D. L. Anderson, *Earthquake Prediction*, Science, May 11, 1973 Vol. 180, No. 4086

Shepard, Macdonald, and Cox, *Tsunami of April 1, 1946*, from *Bulletin of the Scripps Institution of Oceanography*, Vol. V No. 6

GENERAL HAWAIIAN HISTORY

Gavan Daws, *Shoal of Time, A History of the Hawaiian Islands*, HI, UH. Press, 1968

David W. Forbes and Thomas K. Kunichika, *Hilo 1825-1925: A Century of Paintings and Drawings*, HI, LHMM, 1983

Charles F. Gallagher and Dana Levy, *Hawaii and its Gods*, HI, Weatherhill/Kapa, 1975

Hawaiian Almanac and Annual, HI, Thos. G. Thrum, Publisher, 1880, 1896, 1898

D. H. Hicks & Co, *The Hawaiian Kingdom, Statistical and Commercial Directory, 1880-1881*, CA, D.H. Hicks & Co, 1882

Edward Joesting, *Hawaii, An Uncommon History*, NY, W.W. Norton & Co, Inc, 1972

Mary H. Krout, *Hawaii and a Revolution*, NY, Dodd Mead & Co., 1898

Ralph S. Kuykendall & A. Grove Day, *Hawaii: A History*, NJ, Prentice-Hall, 1948

Ralph S. Kuykendall, *The Hawaiian Kingdom, 1778-1854*, HI, U.H. Press, 1968

George F. Nellist, ed, *The Story of Hawaii and Its Builders*, HI, Honolulu Star-Bulletin, 1925

Mary Kawena Pūku'i & Samuel H. Elbert, *Hawaiian Dictionary*, HI, UH Press, 1971

Mary Kawena Pūku'i, Samuel H. Elbert & Esther T. Mo'okini, *Place Names of Hawai'i*, HI, UH Press, 1989

Queen Lili'uokalani, *Liliuokalani, Hawaii's Story by Hawaii's Queen*, MA, Lothrop, Lee, Shepard & Co., 1898

Cora Wells Thorpe, *In the Path of the Trade Winds*, NY, G.P. Putnam's Sons, 1924

Lucian Young, *The Boston at Hawaii*, DC, Gibson Printers, 1898

KEY TO ABBREVIATIONS

FP = First Published

LHMM = Lyman House Memorial Museum

THE PRINCIPALS OF HILO BOARDING SCHOOL

(compiled by Nettie Lyman)

1836-1874	Rev. David Belden Lyman
1874-1878	J. Makaimoku Nae'ole
Sept-Dec 1878	Rev. A.O. Forbes
Dec 1878-Apr 1881	W.B. Oleson
Apr-May 1881	Rev. A.O. Forbes
Jun-Dec 1881	Hon. Joseph Nāwahī
Dec 1881-1886	W.B. Oleson
1886-1890	A.W. Burt
1890-1897	Mrs. W.S. Terry
Apr-Jul 1897	Rev. R.K. Baptiste
1897-1922	Levi C. Lyman
1908-1909	Ellen G. Lyman (acting)
1917-1918	George A. Young (acting)
1922-1924	George M. Hargrove
1924-1925	Levi C. Lyman (acting)
Jul 1925-Dec 1927	G.S. Walker
Jan 1928-Jun 1929	Villas Dragoo
Jun 1929-1940	E.A. Lilley

Index

Levi and Nettie Lyman at their 50th wedding anniversary celebration in Hilo in 1947.